FROM PAIN TO PURPOSE

Turning Pain into Power and Purpose

Stephen Barbee

FROM PAIN TO PURPOSE

Published by Krystal Lee Enterprises (KLE Publishing)
Copyright © 2025 by Stephen Barbee. All rights reserved.
Please send comments and questions:

Krystal Lee Enterprises
770-240-0089 Ext. 1
sales@KLEPub.com

To Reach the Author:
Email: stephen@stephenbarbee.com

Web: www.stephenbarbee.com
www.p2pkc.org

Printed in the United States of America.
All rights reserved. No part of this book may be reproduced or transmitted in any form or by any means, electronic or mechanical, including photocopying, recording, or any information storage and retrieval system without written permission of the publisher except for brief quotations used in reviews, written specifically for inclusion in a newspaper, blog, magazine, or academic paper.

ISBN: 978-1-945066-86-3

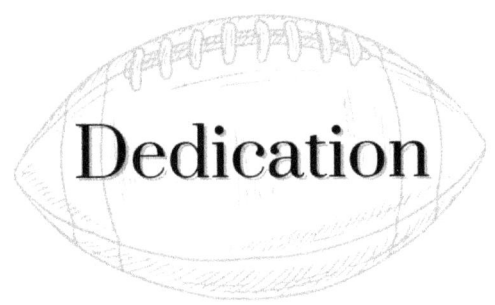

Dedication

To my wife, Deidre Anderson-Barbee

Your love has been one of my life's greatest blessings not because it was easy, but because it was *true*. Real love shows up when it's hard to stay, and that's exactly what you've done.

From our very first call, when you asked me, "What's your story?" You weren't just asking for my past; you were calling out my purpose. That question cracked something open in me. It made me realize I had a story *worth telling*, a story *still being written*. You didn't judge me by the worst chapters I hadn't even told them all yet but you leaned in with compassion, curiosity, and belief. From the beginning, you saw me not just the pain, not just the prison, not just the process but the man, the mission, and the miracle in progress.

You've loved me at my best, yes but more importantly, you loved me at my worst. You covered my brokenness in grace. You saw through the layers of shame, and you dared to speak life into dry places that others had long written off. You stood by me when others walked away, not because I was lovable in that moment, but because **you love like Christ** steadfast, forgiving, powerful, and pure.

You've held space for my healing.
You've warred in prayer when I was too weary to pray for myself.
You've reminded me that grace isn't just a word it's a *way of living*.

You are my answered prayer, the reflection of God's faithfulness in flesh and blood. Your loyalty has been louder than my fear. Your love has outlasted every lie the enemy tried to tell me about my worth. You've not only helped rebuild my confidence you've helped restore my soul.

This book would not exist without your constant presence, patience, and prayers. But more than that **I would not be the man I am without you.**

From pain to purpose…
From silence to story…
From broken to beloved
Thank you for walking with me every step of the way.

I love you always,
Stephen

To **my father, Pastor Leo Barbee Jr.**

You have always been more than a preacher you have been a *pillar*. Your strength, discipline, and faith have shaped the man I continue to become. Even when I strayed far from the truth you lived out daily, your prayers never stopped covering me. You taught me what it means to stand for something, even when the world sits down. Thank you for being a rock when I was crumbling and for loving me enough to never lower your standard, even while extending grace.

To **my mother, Juanita Anne Barbee** *(Sunrise: 1938 – Sunset: 2005)*

You left this world in August of 2005, but your spirit has never left me. I carry your voice, your warmth, and your wisdom with me every single day. I remember your quiet strength the way you comforted without many words, and how your eyes always spoke hope even in my darkest moments. You believed in my potential before I could even see it. This book is as much yours than it is mine. Thank you, Mama, for loving me through it all. May this story honor your legacy.

To Vicky, Jeff, John, Brent, and Brian

You are more than just my siblings—you are part of the foundation God used to hold me up when everything else around me was falling apart.

Each of you, in your own way, has played a role in my redemption. Your love didn't come with conditions it came with a quiet strength, a constant presence, and an unspoken hope that said, *"We're still here."*

Through seasons of silence, shame, and separation, you never turned your backs on me. You prayed, you waited, and you believed often when I couldn't believe for myself.

To **Vicky**, my sister and one of my earliest protectors—thank you for your steady love and the way you've always cared deeply, even through the distance.

To **Jeff**, who paved paths and kept watch I've never forgotten the loyalty and fire that always made me feel covered, even when I was out of control.

To **John**, **Brent**, and **Brian** my brothers who've seen the broken pieces and still stood by me as I picked them up again. Your presence in my life has reminded me of where I come from—and of the man I still strive to become.

You've challenged me to rise, but never condemned me when I fell.
You've reminded me that I carry a name and that it still means something.
You've shown me that *family doesn't forget it fights.*

This journey was never walked alone. I am here today healed, whole, and walking in purpose because **you stood in the gap** for me.

Thank you for your love. Thank you for your covering. And thank you for never letting me go.

With all my love and honor,
Stephen

To my children **Latasha, Stephen, Sherell, Skyelar, and Bria.** And to my grandchildren **Ryeanne, Renae, Brielle, Zya, and Adonis**

Each of you are the heartbeat behind my healing and the reason I continue to press forward. I know I haven't always been the father or grandfather you needed or deserved. There were seasons where my absence spoke louder than my presence, and my pain blocked me from fully showing up. But even in those broken places, my love for you never wavered. I carried you with me in my spirit—through every setback, every prayer, every hard-won step toward becoming the man I was always meant to be.

This book is not just my story—it's part of *your* story, too. Because everything I endured, everything I survived, everything I surrendered to God—it was so I could come back *better*, not just for myself, but for **you**. You are my legacy. You are my joy. You are living proof that grace extends beyond generations.

To my children: Thank you for your patience and your presence. Thank you for giving me another chance to love you with clarity and conviction. I dedicate these words to the unbreakable bond we share no matter the distance, no matter the past.

To my grandchildren: You are the future I longed to see. You are the reason I stand tall today. I pray this story becomes a **blueprint of hope**, a reminder that even if life takes you through dark valleys, you never have to stay there. You were born with promise, on purpose, for purpose.

May my transformation be your testimony.
May my scars become your signposts.
May my comeback become your covering.
And may you always know that Papa loves you and believes in you deeply.

With all my love and all my heart,
Dad / Papa

To **my Aunt Janet Price**,

In a world that often turned its back, you never did. You showed up again and again. Through my struggles, through my incarceration, and through my climb back to the surface, your presence was a quiet miracle. Your loyalty has been louder than any judgment I've ever faced. You extended grace when I couldn't earn it and reminded me that family doesn't flinch in the fire. I love you deeply, and I thank God for your unwavering heart.

This dedication isn't just a page. It's a **thank you letter written in ink**,but lived through blood, tears, and grace. To all who believed in me when I didn't believe in myself—
This is for you.

FROM PAIN TO PURPOSE

Turning Pain into Power and Purpose

Table of Contents

Letter From the Author	11
A Wife's Reflection	15
Introduction	21
Chapter One	25
Chapter Two	29
Chapter Three	35
Chapter Four	45
Chapter Five	65
Chapter Six	83
Chapter Seven	97

Table of Contents

Chapter Eight	109
Chapter Nine	115
Chapter Ten	123
Chapter Eleven	147
Chapter Twelve	163
Chapter Thirteen	207
Chapter Fourteen	213
Chapter Fifteen	263
Chapter Sixteen	273
Chapter Seventeen	277
Chapter Eighteen	283
Closing Reflection	291

A Letter FROM THE AUTHOR

Dear Reader,

If you're holding this book in your hands, I believe it's not by accident. Maybe you found it in a prison library. Maybe someone passed it along to you in a waiting room, a halfway house, or a hospital. Maybe you're searching for answers, or maybe like I once was you're just tired of running.

Wherever you are, whoever you are, I want to speak something over you right now:

You are not alone. You are not too far gone. And your story isn't over.

This book is born from my own brokenness. Not polished, not perfect *but real*. I've lived through nights I didn't think I'd survive. I've wrestled with shame so heavy I couldn't lift my own head. I've sat in prison cells wondering if anyone still believed in me if God still believed in me.

There was a time when I let pain define me. When I believed the lie that my mistakes had canceled my future. Addiction, incarceration, abandonment, loss those things wrote chapters of my life I never planned. But what I came to understand is this:

Pain isn't the period at the end of your sentence it's the comma before your calling.

It was in the lowest, loneliest places that I heard the clearest whisper of God's grace. Not the kind of grace that excuses sin, but the kind that *redeems it*. That restores what was broken and resurrects what was dead. That kind of grace is what I found and it's what I want to share with you.

In these pages, you'll read about the mistakes I made, the people I hurt, the chances I wasted. But you'll also read about second chances, about restoration, about a God who shows up in the middle of your mess and says, "*I'm not done with you yet.*"

My goal in writing this isn't just to tell my story. It's to unlock yours.

Because if you're like me, you've wondered:

- "Is there more to my life than this pain?"
- "Can God really use someone like me?"
- "Am I too broken to be a blessing?"

The answer is yes, yes, and **absolutely not**.

Your scars don't disqualify you they qualify you to reach someone else still bleeding.

Your past doesn't cancel your purpose it *prepares* you for

Letter from the Author

it.

That's what this journey is about. Not just recovery. Not just healing. But **purpose** *on the other side of the pain.*

If you're coming out of prison or just trying to break out of a mental or emotional prison, I pray this book meets you like grace met me in the dark, with a light that won't quit.

So take this journey with me. Walk through the pages. Let the story stir something in your soul. And when you get to the last chapter, I hope you'll realize just like I did that **this isn't the end. It's your beginning.**

Let's walk forward, together.

With gratitude, grace, and purpose,
Stephen Barbee

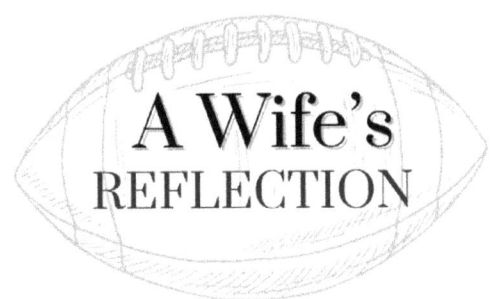

A Wife's Reflection

By Deidre Anderson-Barbee
"The 5 H's + One More H"

When I first heard your voice on **May 24, 2023**, I didn't know the full weight of what God was unfolding—but I knew in my spirit that something sacred was beginning. You spoke with a mix of boldness and vulnerability, sharing your story, your struggles, your surrender, and your second chance with a truthfulness that was raw, humbling, and holy.

But what drew me in wasn't just your testimony. It was your **transparency**, your **tenacity**, and your **trust in God's timing**.

That first question I asked *"What's your story?"* was never small talk.
It was a doorway.
An invitation to see your soul.
To ask: *Can I trust your truth? Will you show me your whole heart?*
And Stephen you did.

By **July 30, 2023**, you weren't just telling your story anymore.
You were writing a new one with me.
You asked me to marry you. And with joy and clarity, I said *yes*.
Not just to you but to **us**.
To the calling. To the covering. To the covenant.
To the journey of loving you forward not just for who you are now,
but for who God is still shaping you to become.

On **December 2, 2023**, we stood before God, our family, and our future,
and I vowed not only to be your *wife* but to be your *witness*.
To your growth.
To your redemption.
To your rise.

We are not perfect but our love is intentional.
Our faith is firm.
And our foundation is **modeled after the 5 H's** plus one more **H:**

Hands

We serve each other.
Not just in big moments, but in the quiet, daily sacrifices.
Washing dishes, holding each other up in prayer, carrying one another burdens.
Your hands, once scarred by pain, now heal others with grace.

 Hearts

We stay emotionally connected, choosing compassion over convenience,
presence over performance.
We love deliberately, even when feelings waver—because covenant isn't based on comfort.
It's based on Christ.

Hugs

We embrace.
Not just physically—but spiritually.
Because in a world that's cold, we've created a refuge in each other's arms.
Our hugs are healing. Our touch is testimony.

Health

We are committed to our wellness—spiritually, emotionally, and physically.
We check in, not just check out.
We pray together. We grow together.
Because **whole love requires whole hearts.**

Honesty

We speak the truth, even when it's uncomfortable.
Not to tear down, but to build up.
Our transparency breeds trust, and our honesty deepens intimacy.
You taught me that love without truth is fragile. But love with truth is *freeing*.

Humor (Our "Plus One")

And then—there's this beautiful extra layer:
We laugh.
Oh, how we laugh.
We find joy in the ordinary.
We crack jokes in chaos.
We dance in the kitchen, even though I'm still teaching you to dance.
We tease each other with love and laugh ourselves out of tension.
Because sometimes healing doesn't come in a sermon—it comes in a smile.
And sometimes God's grace shows up not in thunder—but in giggles.
Your laughter is music to me, Stephen.
And your sense of humor reminds me that love should be **light**, not heavy.

Stephen, I've seen every side of you.
Not just the spotlight.
Not just the speaker.
I've seen the man who prays when no one's watching.
Who carries conviction with courage.
Who makes coffee for me in the morning and covers me in prayer at night.
Who cries without restraint because of the depth of you love for all humanity.

I've seen your **scars**—and your **strength**.
I've seen your **humility**—and your **hope**.
You are a leader who listens.
A protector who nurtures.
A man of purpose, not just in public—but in private.

Thank you for choosing me.
Thank you for loving me with clarity, with consistency, with Christ at the center.
Thank you for making me laugh, even when life tries to make me cry.
Thank you for proving that **redemption is real**—and that God's design for marriage still works when two people surrender daily.

I am proud to be your wife.
I believe in our love and in you.
I walk with you—hand in hand,
heart to heart, hope to hope.
Your willingness to boldly share your story, has allowed me and so many others to share theirs.
That is a gift that is like no other so keep speaking.

Forever, with love and laughter,
Deidre Anderson-Barbee
Your Wife. Your Partner. Your Prayer Warrior. Your Best Friend in Faith… and in Fun.

Introduction

FROM PAIN TO PURPOSE

My life journey highlights my transformation from a star athlete to a person battling addiction, incarceration, and eventually becoming an advocate for change.

As I walked into the courtroom, the weight of every choice, every mistake, pressed down on my shoulders like an anchor. The air felt thick with expectation, the quiet shuffle of papers, the low murmur of voices – all of it seemed surreal, like I was standing outside of myself, watching this moment unfold.

"All rise." The voice boomed across the room, snapping me back to reality. Judge John W. Lungstrum entered, his presence both commanding and calm. I stood with my lawyer, Stephen Switzer, by my side. My heart pounded in my chest, and my palms were damp with a nervous sweat. It was a strange mix of emotions – fear, regret, and a solemn acceptance of what was to come.

Stephen Barbee

The judge's eyes were steady as he began to speak. I felt them, though I couldn't meet his gaze for long. "Mr. Barbee, I realize you come from a great family," he said, his words echoing through the quiet room. My eyes drifted to where my father, step-mother, and sister sat. They were a picture of resilience and grace, even in the midst of this nightmare. I knew the toll this had taken on them, and the guilt weighed heavily on me. *I let them down,* I thought. The judge continued, reminding me of the opportunities I'd had, the successes I'd once known. Football, education, and a career – all squandered because of the choices I made.

He paused, and I could feel every eye in the courtroom on me, the walls almost closing in. "Society says I must deem you a sentence. I pray, Mr. Barbee, that whatever demons you're dealing with, you face them after I render this sentence."

The room was still, the air thick with anticipation. The floor beneath my feet felt unsteady as the reality of the moment settled in. The judge's words echoed in my mind, and for a second, everything was quiet, everything slowed down. I swallowed hard, steadying myself for what I knew was coming.

"Do you have any closing statements before I render your sentence?" His voice broke the silence, and I realized this was it – my last chance to speak. I took a deep breath, feeling the weight of every word before I spoke.

"Your Honor," I began, my voice steadier than I expected. "I recognize that I have broken the law, not just several times, but over the last few years." My voice wavered slightly, but I pressed on. "This is my fate in life as I stand before you – a former football All-American, a father, a son, and, most of all, a U.S. citizen." I took another breath, glancing at my family, then back at the judge. "Your Honor, I take full responsibility for my actions for breaking the law. Whatever sentence you render, I, Stephen Barbee, deserve it."

A wave of emotion surged through me – shame, relief, sorrow – as I finished speaking. I could feel the eyes of my family on me, their silent prayers and hopes hanging in the air.

The judge nodded, his face unreadable. "Thank you, Mr. Barbee, for your statement of truth and honesty." He adjusted his glasses, and I braced myself for the inevitable. "At this time, I sentence you, Stephen Barbee, to 70 months in federal prison." My stomach lurched, but I stood firm. "Upon completion of your federal sentence, you will be required to be on court supervision for 60 months."

The words landed heavily, final, and unchangeable. The courtroom remained still, the weight of it all sunk into every corner of the room. I nodded, my body numb. This was it – my reality, my sentence. Yet, even in that moment of darkness, there was a strange peace, a calm acceptance of the consequences I had brought upon myself.

"Thank you, Mr. Barbee," the judge said, his voice softer now. I turned toward my family, their faces filled with love and sadness. I knew this was the beginning of a long road, but I also knew, deep down, that this wasn't the end of my story. It was the start of something different – a chance to face those demons, to rebuild, to rise again.

Chapter ONE

THE RISE: A PROMISING START

The Foundations of Faith and Family

The 13th of July, 1964, marked the beginning of my journey in this world. I was born Leo Stephen Barbee to my parents, Leo Barbee Jr. and Juanita Ann (Terry) Barbee. I was the third of what would eventually be six children, part of a family deeply rooted in faith and tradition. My father, a man of conviction, set the tone for our household. His reverence for God was unwavering, and he lived out his beliefs through daily actions and monumental decisions.

A life-changing decision that defined his life was the day he declined an offer to play professional baseball with the St. Louis Cardinals to remain with us and be an active pastor, father, and husband. For many, this

Chapter One

opportunity would have been a dream come true. To my father, however, the idea of breaking his commitment to worship and serve God on Sundays was unimaginable. Today, as of this writing, my father has been preaching the gospel for an astounding 66 years, a testament to his dedication and strength of faith.

In **1968**, my family moved from **Joplin, Missouri** to **Wichita Falls, Texas**, where my father became the pastor of Pilgrim Rest Missionary Baptist Church. This move marked the beginning of my journey into athletics, and the 1970s were transformative years for me, both spiritually and athletically. My younger brothers—John, Brent, and Brian—were born during this time, each adding to the rich fabric of our family life in Texas.

It was in Texas that I accepted Jesus Christ as my personal Savior. I remember vividly my baptism at Pilgrim Rest Missionary Baptist Church, a significant moment in my early years. As my father pastored there for a few years before moving on to Shiloh Missionary Baptist Church, my faith grew alongside my curiosity about the world. Sundays were dedicated to church, with morning and afternoon services, Sunday school, and Wednesday night Bible studies. These moments weren't just religious routines; they were times for me to cultivate a deeper understanding of the Bible and cultivate a desire to learn more about God's Word.

Sports began to capture my attention as I played with the other kids in our neighborhood. We were just young boys getting into occasional mischief, but sports offered me a way to channel my energy. My earliest memory of kindergarten was attending school at a Seventh-Day Adventist institution, where I met my lifelong

The Rise: A Promising Start

friend, **Dennis Turner**. Even now, decades later, that bond remains strong.

Life in **Wichita Falls** was punctuated by memorable trips with my father as he traveled to various churches in Texas to preach. I was often by his side, sitting in the front seat, taking in the sermons as he delivered the Gospel. One of the most unforgettable moments from those years happened when I was just four years old—a moment of panic for my parents and a lesson in trust for me.

We were on a trip, my father driving through **Tulsa, Oklahoma**, with my mother resting in the passenger seat. It was late at night, and my mother was pregnant with my twin siblings, **Brent and Brian**. I had been placed under the watchful care of my grandmother in **Springfield, Missouri**, while my older siblings stayed back in Texas for school. As we stopped at a gas station to refuel, I innocently asked my mother for permission to use the restroom. She nodded, half-asleep, and I slipped out of the car. What I didn't realize was that, in the tiredness of the moment, my parents would drive off without me.

After finishing in the restroom, I stepped outside to find the car—and my family—gone. I was just a small boy, alone, scared, and standing under the fluorescent lights of a gas station. The station attendant, noticing I had been left behind, grew concerned. He believed I had been abandoned and promptly called the police. Not long after, a police officer arrived and took me to the local station, where I sat waiting, bewildered and unsure of what would happen next.

Chapter One

    Meanwhile, miles down the road, my mother suddenly woke up and asked my father, "Did Stevie get back in the car?" In that instant, panic set in. My father frantically pulled the car over and searched every corner, under every seat, but I was nowhere to be found. The drive back to the gas station must have felt like the longest journey of their lives. While I waited at the police station, the officers did their best to comfort me. They handed me a **Dr. Pepper** and a **Butterfingers**, a small act of kindness that, even at my young age, helped me feel a little less scared. When they asked where I was going, I confidently told them, "Springfield, Missouri." They seemed impressed that I not only knew our destination but also remembered my father's phone numbers—both to our house and the church. In my heart, I never doubted that my dad would come back for me.

    When they arrived, they were relieved to find me safe and sound at the police station, thanks to the quick-thinking attendant. That night, I learned just how much I was loved, and it became one of the family stories told for years to come. I was filled with a sense of joy and relief. I knew my dad would never leave me behind, and seeing him step through that station door was all the reassurance I needed.

THE BIRTH OF THE ATHLETE

People often ask me, "Where did you get the heart to be such an athlete?" Looking back, it's clear that growing up in **Texas**, a state famous for its fierce dedication to sports—football, basketball, and baseball—had a lot to do with it. My first team sport was baseball, and our team name was the **Wolverines**. In fact, no matter what sport I played—whether it was football or basketball—our team was always called the Wolverines. It was a name that carried a sense of strength and unity, and it became a big part of my early identity as an athlete.

I'll never forget the coach who believed in me early on, **Coach Thom**. He saw something in me before I even saw it in myself. At first, I was just another young player on the team, trying to find my place. I started out as a **running back**, using my speed to break through the defense. But one day, Coach Thom made a game-changing

Chapter Two

decision—he moved me to **quarterback**. It didn't take long for me to realize that the quarterback had a unique power over the team. I was the one calling the plays and deciding the direction of the game. At that young age, I began to understand what it meant to lead.

I still remember calling out plays like **18 Power Sweep** and **19 Power Sweep**, knowing they were designed for me to carry the ball. Sometimes, just for fun, I'd switch myself from quarterback to tight end, call a passing play, and then catch the ball myself. The thrill of running down the field with the ball in my hands and scoring touchdowns was electrifying.

Living in **Wichita Falls, Texas**, gave me countless opportunities to develop as a football, baseball, and basketball player. My natural talent, combined with the competitive spirit of Texas sports culture, helped shape me into the athlete I would become. But it wasn't just about the games. One of the most important parts of my childhood was my friendship with **Dennis Turner**. Dennis and I were almost the same age—born just three months apart—and our bond was built on a shared love for sports. He played tight end, and together, we created unforgettable memories on the field.

Today, our friendship remains strong, a testament to the lifelong connections forged during those early years of competition and camaraderie. Some of my fondest memories involve my good friend **Dennis Turner**. We spent countless hours together on the field, Dennis playing tight end and me switching from **quarterback** to **running back**—and occasionally tight end myself. Whenever I made the switch, Dennis had to move to another position, and he never complained. We were a team, in every sense of the word, always having each other's backs, no matter the challenge.

Our games were intense, especially against the local teams in **Wichita Falls, Texas**. There was **Little League football**, and we faced off against teams like the **Leopards** and **Vikings**—and those teams were no joke. I'll never forget the **Leopards**. They wore **blue shirts** and **silver helmets**, and their entire lineup, from the head coach down to the water boy, was almost entirely Black. Every year, they put it on us, and I mean **really** put it on us. The Leopards were a powerhouse, and going up against them was like facing giants.

But there were also moments of triumph, like when we got to play teams from **Sheppard Air Force Base** and the **Missiles** and **Rockets**. We had a special kind of pride every time we left the base with a victory. Then there was the **Longhorns**, a team that was made up of **Mexican-American players**. While they may not have been the strongest football team, they were incredible athletes, especially when it came to soccer. They played with heart, and even though football wasn't their game, they had my respect.

Basketball was another love of mine. I remember going down to the **Boys Club**, where they'd lower the goals to **eight feet** because most of us weren't tall enough for the standard hoops. Of course, I was still playing for the Wolverines, and Dennis was always on my team. Those games were intense and fun, with short goals that made for exciting plays. In **baseball**, too, we were teammates. I played **catcher**, and Dennis was our **pitcher**. I remember one game so clearly. Dennis was throwing the ball so hard that I had to call a timeout,

Chapter Two

walk up to the pitcher's mound, and say, "Hey Dennis, man, slow down on that fastball! You're hurting my hand!" That moment still makes me laugh when I think about it.

Those were the days of **teamwork**, **camaraderie**, and learning what it meant to win—and lose—together. But the lessons weren't always easy. I'll never forget one football game where we had just been beaten badly. I was sitting on the bench, crying, feeling the sting of defeat. My mom and dad were sitting in the car behind the fence, right next to my bench. My dad called out to me, "Stevie, go shake those players' hands. If you don't, you'll never play football again."

At that moment, I didn't want to. I was upset, hurt, and frustrated. But my dad's words echoed in my head. He was teaching me that no matter how tough the loss, sportsmanship mattered more than winning. Reluctantly, I got up, wiped my tears, and shook the other players' hands. That lesson stayed with me throughout my life—always show respect to your opponents, win or lose.

It was one of those pivotal moments that taught me about grace, humility, and what it means to carry yourself with dignity, even in defeat. Wichita Falls, Texas, is where my love for sports really began to take root. It's where I first started learning about **football**, **baseball**, and **basketball**—and about what it meant to both win and lose. Back then, we didn't have specialized leagues for the younger kids like **T-ball**.

At the age of six, I played regular baseball, and I remember how much I **hated to lose**. No one wanted to play **catcher**, so I volunteered for the position. I don't remember much about the season or the records we held, but what stands out most was my desire to compete and contribute to the team in any way I could.

In football, I played for the **Wolverines**—and those were some of the most fun times of my early life. It wasn't uncommon for me to keep the ball and run around the right or left end, often calling my own plays. My brother **Jeff** used to tease me, calling me a "**ball hog**," but I didn't mind. I was determined to help the team win, even if it meant shouldering more of the responsibility. I remember our team colors—**black and gold**—and I also remember the sting of missing the playoffs by just one or two wins during a couple of seasons. Despite those setbacks, I was proud to receive the **Best Back award** and the **team's Most Valuable Player award** after one of those seasons. Those awards reinforced my growing confidence as an athlete.

It wasn't just about sports with Dennis and I. My older brother Jeff played a major role in my life, especially during our time in Wichita Falls. We lived in the **East Linwood neighborhood,** and one of our regular routines involved going to the **Boys Club** every Saturday morning. My brother Jeff and I would spend the entire day there, playing sports, hanging out, and just being kids. Jeff always looked out for me, protecting me even when I was in the wrong, and that sense of brotherhood stuck with me throughout my life.

One of my favorite memories with Jeff was when he had a **paper route**. His route took him by this open field with a **horse** in it. One day, Jeff, being the adventurous type, decided to set that horse free. Not only did he set the horse free, but he also rode it to finish his paper route

Chapter Two

that day. It was classic Jeff—bold, fearless, and always ready for the next adventure. He was my protector and my hero, and that moment is just one example of the fun and rebellious spirit he brought to my childhood.

Chapter THREE

THE MOVE TO KANSAS CITY

As much as I loved playing football, basketball, and baseball in Wichita Falls, life took a turn in **1975** when my family moved to **Kansas City, Missouri**. My father, always dedicated to his calling, was in line to become the pastor of **Park Avenue Missionary Baptist Church**, but we didn't get the church. It was a tough blow, but not just for him—for me too. That was the first time I can remember **not being able to play football**. It was like a part of me was missing, and that fall season felt incredibly long without the game I had grown to love.

In Wichita Falls, I had always dreamed of moving up to the **Midget League**, where the games were played **at night under the lights**. There was something magical about those games. But by the time I would've been old enough, we were already preparing for the move to Kansas City. Looking back, it's one of those "what could

Chapter Three

have been" moments. I never got to play midget football in Texas, and the absence of football in my life that year left a void.

Yet, even when things seemed uncertain, my family was always there to support me. My **Uncle Tommy**, who was always looking out for me, found out about a **basketball league** at the **Boys and Girls Club**. It was through him that I ended up playing for the **Art Bunker Volkswagen team** in a league called **Biddy Basketball**. That season turned out to be **a great year for me**, not just because I got to continue playing sports but because I was able to find my stride on the basketball court.

I met a lot of good friends in that league, although their names escape me now. What I do remember, though, is the **trip to Chicago** for the **Itty Bitty International Tournament**. That trip is etched in my memory. We took the **Amtrak train**, traveling overnight to Chicago. It felt like an adventure, riding through the night with my teammates, excited for the games ahead.

When we arrived, we stayed at the **Boys and Girls Club** on the **west side of Chicago**. The anticipation was high, but when we took to the court, we quickly realized we were in for a tough challenge. These Chicago boys were **tall—5'10", 5'11", and 6 feet tall**—and we were still just 11 and 12 years old. As soon as we saw the size of the competition, we knew we were going to get beat. Boy, did we get beat—**twice**.

Despite the losses, it was an experience I wouldn't trade for anything. My **Uncle Kenny** even came to watch the games; having family there made it feel special. We didn't come away with any wins, but the trip taught me

The Move to Kansas City

a lot about competing on a bigger stage, **resilience,** and dealing with **defeat**. Those lessons would stick with me for years to come.

It was great playing basketball in Kansas City, but that summer, I had the opportunity to dive back into baseball, this time with Raytown Bank in Kansas City, Missouri. It wasn't the best season—far from it. I played almost every position: catcher, first base, pitcher, second base, left field, right field, and center field. The reason I got moved around so much was because, quite frankly, we couldn't win.

We ended up going 0-16—sixteen straight losses. I'll never forget that feeling of defeat. It was a tough and humbling summer for me, but in the middle of that struggle, I made a promise to myself: I would never be part of a defeated season again. That drive, that burning desire to never taste that kind of losing streak again stuck with me as I grew in both baseball and football.

It was a season I will never forget. Game after game, we walked off the field with nothing to show for our effort but frustration and disappointment. It was a tough and humbling summer, one that tested my love for the game and my belief in myself. I had always been competitive, always hungry to win, but this was something different. This was an extended taste of failure, a reminder that effort alone doesn't always translate into victory.

After that final loss, as we packed up our gear in silence, I made a promise to myself: I would never be part of a defeated season again. That drive, that burning desire to never experience that kind of losing streak again,

Chapter Three

stuck with me as I grew in both baseball and football.

But that 0-16 season was more than just about sports. It was a defining moment that shaped how I approached every setback in life. At the time, it felt like failure, but looking back, it was a test of resilience. It taught me a lesson I would carry into the battles ahead—through struggles with addiction, incarceration, and the process of rebuilding my life.

Losing every game that season forced me to confront the sting of defeat head-on. It would have been easy to accept losing as my reality, to sink into frustration and blame. But instead, I vowed that I would do whatever it took to never feel that helpless again. That promise wasn't just about sports—it was about life. I learned that setbacks are temporary, but my response to them defines my future.

This mindset became my foundation. When addiction tried to claim my life, when incarceration threatened to break my spirit, and when rebuilding seemed impossible, I leaned on the same fire that was ignited during that winless season. I refused to accept defeat, even when my circumstances screamed otherwise.

The greatest lesson I took from that season was that losing doesn't make you a loser—quitting does. Every setback is an opportunity to grow stronger, to develop the kind of perseverance that transforms failure into fuel for the next victory. That's a lesson I carry with me to this day, in sports, in life, and in my mission to help others overcome their own struggles.

As my sports and athletic career were beginning

The Move to Kansas City

to take shape, life shifted once again. In 1976, my dad accepted the call to become the pastor of 9th Street Missionary Baptist Church in Lawrence, Kansas. This meant starting over—again. New town, new school, and new friends. But it also meant a new opportunity to prove myself, especially on the athletic field. Moving to Lawrence felt like entering unknown territory, but over time, it became a place we would call home.

West Junior High School was my first stop in Lawrence. I was the new kid on the block, and it wasn't easy to break into established circles. I didn't have many friends at first, but there were a couple of guys I clicked with right away—Scott Watson and Delmar White. We bonded over football and basketball, and they became my closest friends during that time. We didn't just play sports together; we did almost everything together.

Friday nights were for hanging out, and our spot was Hillcrest. We would head to the bowling alley, sometimes playing a few rounds, but more often, we just chilled. Afterward, we'd make our way to the arcade, burning through quarters on video games, and eventually, we'd end up at the skating rink. That's how we spent our weekends—carefree and full of fun.

On Mondays and Tuesdays, we'd meet up on our bikes and cruise over to Michigan Avenue. Biking together was part of our routine, and we always had to coordinate what we were wearing. It might seem trivial now, but back then, it mattered! We'd joke around, asking each other, "What are you wearing today?" We had our own little fashion code—gray T-shirts with blue jeans or white T-shirts with black jeans. It wasn't just about clothes, though; it was about the bond we shared.

Chapter Three

The friendships I built in those early days at West Junior High weren't just about sports. It was about sticking together, navigating a new place, and finding our own sense of belonging. Those guys were more than just teammates—they were my first real friends in Lawrence, and they made the transition easier for me. And, of course, we played ball—whether it was on the field or on the court, we always found a way to compete.

Playing basketball at West Junior High School was an unforgettable experience, not just because of the games but because of the camaraderie we shared. Scott Watson, Delmar White, and I were the only Black players on the team both in eighth and ninth grade, and that alone created a bond among us. We stood out, not just for our skills, but for who we were, and we leaned on each other. We didn't let that pressure get to us—we embraced it, and it only made us tighter as friends and as teammates.

Off the court, life in Lawrence was just as memorable. Skating was *the* thing to do back in the day. Everyone went, and if you were lucky, you'd stay for both the first and second sessions. The rink was more than a place to skate—it was where we all gathered, hung out, and had fun. I'll never forget one particular night when Jeff, my brother, wanted to go skating so bad that we broke into our piggy banks. We scraped together 175 pennies each—yeah, pennies—and headed to the skating rink.

I can still see Jeff at the window, emptying his pockets and pouring out his pile of pennies onto the counter. The attendant, bless his patience, counted every single one. Once Jeff was in, I followed behind with my 175 pennies ready, but the guy just shook his head. "I'm not

The Move to Kansas City

counting these," he said. "If you want to skate that bad, go on in." And just like that, we got in with a pocket full of pennies, eager to skate the night away. It's a small thing, but moments like that stick with you.

Then there was that night with Tony Owens. We had a plan—one that involved sneaking off to hang out with some female friends. Of course, we stayed at their place the whole night, but when I got home the next morning, I had to think fast. My mom asked me where I had been, and I, of course, lied and told her I had spent the night at Tony's house. "What'd you and Tony do?" she asked. "We went skating," I replied confidently, telling her how we stayed for both sessions, just like I'd done so many times before.

But my mom had that sixth sense only mothers have. Without missing a beat, she grabbed the morning newspaper, tossed it to me, and said, "Skating, huh?" Right there on the front page: *Tornado wipes out skating rink.* I was caught. I had no idea there had been a tornado, let alone that it hit the rink. She didn't have to say much after that—her look said it all.

That's the thing about my mom. She always knew when we were telling the truth and when we were trying to pull one over on her. No matter how clever we thought we were, she was always one step ahead. It was like she had a built-in lie detector. It didn't matter how good of a story I came up with; she'd always catch me. Looking back, I can laugh about it now, but back then, her intuition seemed almost supernatural.

The summer of 1976 in Lawrence, Kansas, was one of the most memorable summers for me, not only be-

Chapter Three

cause it marked my first time playing baseball there but because it taught me lessons that would stick with me for life. I got drafted by VFW, the Veterans of Foreign Wars team, and though I initially played on their minor league team, Breakfast Optimist, it was a new beginning for me. Playing at Holcom Complex was special, and I found myself competing against teams like Rotary, Royals, and Dairy Queen—names that are still vivid in my mind.

One of the best parts about playing for VFW was meeting Frank Heck, even though our first encounter wasn't exactly smooth. Frank played for the Wakarusa basketball team, and we almost came to blows during a game on the basketball court. It was one of those heated moments where pride and competition collided, but that rough start turned into one of the most important friendships of my life. Frank and I became inseparable. We not only played baseball together in Lawrence, but we also played football at Lawrence High School and eventually went on to play baseball at Highland Community College. Frank became more than just a teammate—he was a brother to me.

When I look back at that time, playing sports shaped more than just my athletic abilities. It taught me discipline, conditioned me mentally and physically, and helped me learn what it means to be a team player. Sports gave me a new lens through which I could view life, helping me understand the value of hard work, teamwork, and perseverance.

One particular memory that stands out is a football game between West Junior High and Central Junior

The Move to Kansas City

High. We had been on a losing streak at West, so the game against Central felt like a make-or-break moment. It was one of those chilly nights when everything was on the line. The moment came in the second quarter—I remember taking the ball and scoring on the very first play from two yards out. The crowd erupted, but the job wasn't done. Brian Cox had to follow up with a crucial two-point conversion, and just like that, West beat Central.

I'll never forget what JD Clevenger said after that win: "The win has been long overdue, so long in fact that we don't know how to act." That game, that win, was a reminder of what persistence and belief could achieve. It wasn't just about the victory on the field—it was a statement that we were capable of turning things around, no matter how tough the circumstances. Those memories of playing football, baseball, and basketball during junior high school were eventful because of the friendships, their unique challenges, and learning how to navigate life through the lens of sports. Every game, every practice, and every win or loss became a stepping stone that shaped who I am today.

Another memorable moment was playing basketball with Carl Boldra, a close friend who later played high school and college football with me. We had some incredible games, especially the one against Shawnee Heights. Carl was on fire that day—he scored a game-high of 16 points, grabbed nine rebounds, and set up three key baskets down the stretch. We won that game 62-49, and though our B team lost 33-26, it was a victory that brought us closer as a team. I remember Coach Gilliam saying, "Carl's just one of those guys who was in the right place at the right time." That was Carl—always

Chapter Three

dependable, always making the smart plays.

Jeff Harkins and I both chipped in with 10 points each, and Preston Boyer dominated the boards, pulling down 12 rebounds. That win brought our record to 6-3. Another unforgettable game was when we faced Logan Junior High. Carl again led the charge, scoring 22 points and pulling down a staggering 19 rebounds. I had a solid performance, too, with 14 points, while Joe Schulte contributed as well. Jeff Harkins added 8 points and grabbed 12 rebounds, securing our fifth straight victory of the season. That game was a testament to how much we had grown as a team.

Carl Boldra, Joe Schulte, Scott Watson, Delmar White—these were the guys who made junior high basketball memorable. And, of course, receiving my first letter in 1979, in football, basketball, and track, was a moment of pride. It marked a milestone in my athletic journey and reinforced the idea that hard work pays off.

MAKING A NAME FOR MYSELF

Lawrence, Kansas, was home to only one high school at the time—Lawrence High School—one of the largest and most competitive schools in the state. Transitioning from West Junior High to Lawrence High felt like stepping onto a bigger stage, and it pushed me to continue growing as an athlete. The lessons I learned playing at West, especially with guys like Carl and Jeff, laid the foundation for the rest of my athletic career.

Attending Lawrence High School, one of the largest schools in Kansas, was an intimidating experience at first. The sheer size of the school felt overwhelming, but I knew that sports would help me find my place. Football, especially, became my avenue for building confidence and adjusting to this new environment.

I vividly remember one of our most exciting games

Chapter Four

against Olathe. We came out on top, winning 24-6 on our home field. Mark Henderson had a standout performance, scoring two touchdowns and three conversions. I scored on a three-yard run and a 30-yard touchdown in the first half. The game started in our favor as we struck first with a determined one-yard touchdown run. Although our conversion attempt fell short, we held a narrow 8-6 lead early on. The intensity on the field was undeniable—both teams knew what was at stake, and neither was willing to back down.

As the second quarter unfolded, Henderson found his rhythm, bulldozing his way into the end zone for a four-yard touchdown. This time, we capitalized on the conversion, pushing our advantage to 16-6. But the opposing team wasn't going down without a fight. They mounted a strong defensive stand, shutting down our next few drives and keeping the game within reach. The pressure was mounting, and we knew we needed a spark to maintain control.

At halftime, the locker room buzzed with energy and urgency. Coach pulled us in close, his voice cutting through the tension.

"Listen up! We started strong, but this game is far from over," he said, scanning each of us with unwavering intensity. "They're gonna come out hungry in the second half, looking to take momentum. But we've got the heart, the fight, and the talent to finish this. Stick to the fundamentals. Hit hard, play smart, and trust each other. We've worked too damn hard to let this slip now."

Then he turned to Henderson, his tone firm yet encouraging. "Keep running like you own that field. They

Making a Name for Myself

can't stop you unless you stop yourself."

He looked at Boldra next. "When the opportunity's there, take the shot. Stay poised, stay sharp."

As we broke the huddle, the team roared in unison, fired up for the second half.

The third quarter was a grind. Our defense held strong, denying the opponent any chance to close the gap, but our offense struggled to break through their adjustments. The tension in the stadium grew with each passing minute.

Then, in the final quarter, the moment came. Boldra dropped back, eyes scanning the field. Henderson broke free from his defender, cutting towards the end zone. With a well-timed throw, Boldra connected with him on a perfect 10-yard strike, the ball landing in his hands as he crossed the goal line. The crowd erupted. That touchdown sealed it. Victory was ours.

We left that field battered, exhausted—but victorious. It was a game of grit, a battle of wills, and we had come out on top.

The game was close for a while, but in the third quarter, we broke it open. After scoring early on with a one-yard run, although the conversion attempt failed, we led 8-6. Henderson then powered through with another four-yard touchdown run and conversion, giving us a 16-6 lead. Carl Boldra connected with Henderson once again in the final quarter on a 10-yard touchdown pass, sealing our victory.

Another unforgettable game was against Topeka

Chapter Four

High. That match was hard-fought, and the score was tied at 6 early in the fourth quarter. We took the lead on a one-yard sneak by Mike Carmody, and from there, momentum shifted in our favor. Fred Hunter came through with a game-changing 57-yard fumble return, effectively putting the game out of reach. Our first touchdown came in the second quarter when Carl Boldra threw a 25-yard pass to me, and we never looked back after that.

The Calm Before the Storm: Game Day at Lawrence High

The locker room was quiet. Not the kind of forced quiet, but a silence that carried weight—a focused, electric stillness. The only sounds were the occasional shuffle of cleats against the tile floor, the rustling of jerseys being adjusted, and the soft, steady breathing of a team on the edge of battle.

We sat on the wooden benches, heads down, lacing up our black shoes—scuffed, worn, battle-tested. The black helmets sat beside us, glossy and proud, reflecting the dim locker room light. The contrast was striking—the white pants against the deep black of our jerseys and helmets. This was more than a uniform. It was tradition. It was an identity. It was Lawrence High football.

Coach Freeman stood at the front, arms folded, scanning the room. He didn't need to yell. He didn't need theatrics. He just *was*. His presence alone commanded our attention, our respect. And in that hushed room, before the storm of the game, he would remind us:

"Boys, regardless if we win or lose, the sun will

rise tomorrow."

A simple truth, grounding us. It wasn't just about the game—it was about how we carried ourselves, how we played for the name across our chest, how we honored those who came before us.

Then came the walk. Cleats clicking against the concrete, a rhythm that grew in intensity as we stepped onto the bus. No words were spoken. No music. No distractions. Just silence. Each player locked in his own world, mentally running through the first snap, the first hit, the first moment we'd leave it all on the field. The bus rumbled forward, carrying a team bound together in that stillness, bound by years of tradition and expectation.

Outside, the night crept in, the stadium lights of the opposing field glowing in the distance like a beacon calling us to battle. The moment the bus doors hissed open, the silence broke. Not with words, not with shouts—but with purpose. Black helmets strapped tight, hands clenched into fists, eyes burning with focus.

And then, as we hit the field, Coach's voice rang out one last time.

"Hell's bells, boys!"

And just like that, the silence was gone. The war had begun.

Coach Bill Freeman's influence on our team was profound. He was the kind of coach who not only emphasized physical conditioning but also taught us what it meant to play as a cohesive unit. He pushed us to be

Chapter Four

better, and those lessons extended far beyond the football field.

Football at Lawrence High was about more than just victories. It was a place where I grew, found my identity, and learned the value of teamwork and resilience. Each game was a stepping stone in my journey, preparing me for the challenges that lay ahead.

Playing for Lawrence High in those days was truly an incredible experience. I remember the excitement of my first varsity start, facing Junction City at Haskell Stadium, a place that holds so many cherished memories. The atmosphere on Friday nights was electric, with five to six thousand fans in the stands, all there to support the Lions. Although I didn't contribute much to that game—just six carries for 20 yards—the thrill of playing under the lights for the varsity team as a junior was something I'll never forget.

Lawrence High was known for dominating the field, especially against smaller schools. One of our biggest victories that season was against Topeka West, where we shut them out 35-0. I had a special moment during that game, scoring my first-ever varsity touchdown on a three-yard run. That feeling of crossing into the end zone, even for a short run, was unforgettable. My five carries for 21 yards that night may not have been the most impressive stats, but that touchdown was a major milestone for me.

Our team was unstoppable that season, going undefeated and blowing out teams left and right. Shawnee Mission West, North, South, and Northwest all fell to us, as did Topeka High. Each game further cemented Lawrence High's reputation as a football powerhouse, and I was proud to be part of such a talented and cohesive unit. Every win added to the legacy of our team, and being a contributor, even as a junior, felt like being part of something much bigger.

Those memories of the 1979 season, the camaraderie, the thrill of victory, and the lessons learned on and off the field are still vivid to me. It was a time of growth, not only as an athlete but also as a person.

My senior year at Lawrence High School was one of the most memorable times of my life, filled with unforgettable moments both on and off the field. Being a Chesty Lion during that 1981 season was something special, a year that would go down in history as one of dominance and pride. We went undefeated, beating every school in the Sunflower District with precision, passion, and power.

I'll never forget our first district game that season against Highland Park. We were only up 7-0 at halftime, and it felt like we were underperforming. Coach Bill Freeman, known for his fiery motivational style, walked into the locker room, looked at us, and simply said, "Boys, you stink," before walking right out. That silence was deafening. The air felt heavy until Coach Nanny Dover came in, grabbed our manager, Andy Coleman, spun him around, and said one word: "Lawrence." He pointed to the "L" on Andy's chest and asked, "Boys, what does this mean?" That was all it took. We knew what we had to do. We went back out there and blew out Highland Park in the second half, securing a victory that set the tone for the rest of the season!

Chapter Four

The district games against the Topeka schools were also hard-fought battles. Playing Topeka High and Topeka West was never easy, but we pulled through, showcasing the discipline and grit that Lawrence High football was known for. We beat Topeka West in a tough contest, but it was our final home game against Topeka High that truly stood out.

Topeka High had a running back named John Kendrick, who had been making headlines all season. He got on statewide TV before the season began and confidently predicted that he would rush for 1,500 yards. By the time we faced them in the last game of the year, Kendrick had racked up 1,449 yards—just 51 yards shy of his goal. The entire week leading up to the game, Coach Freeman drilled into us the importance of containing Kendrick. In fact, Coach Freeman, with his thick, recognizable hair, made a bold promise to the team: "If we hold him under 51 yards, I'll shave my head."

That game against Topeka High was intense. The stakes were high, not just for Kendrick's yardage but for our pride and undefeated season. We were determined not to let him hit that 1,500-yard mark. I remember the defense playing lights out, and every time Kendrick touched the ball, we swarmed him. I personally had four carries for 20 yards that night, but the true victory was on the defensive side. Kendrick ended up with just 16 carries for 46 yards, falling short of his goal.

On Monday, after the game, Coach Freeman walked into the locker room wearing a ball cap, and we all knew what was coming. With a grin, he pulled off his cap, revealing a freshly shaved head. He was a man of his word, and we had delivered. That moment cemented the bond we had as a team and showed just how much pride we took in our Lawrence High legacy.

We finished the season 9-0 as Sunflower League Champions, and it was a testament to the hard work, camaraderie, and coaching that shaped us as athletes and young men. That senior year wasn't just about football; it was about becoming your best self and being willing to give that to others for the team to benefit. That brotherhood stuck with me throughout my life. Lawrence High School football in 1981 was something extraordinary, and I'm proud to have been part of it.

Going into the league playoffs that year, there was a lot of buzz surrounding Lawrence High and Shawnee Mission Northwest. We were ranked first, and they were ranked second, which had everyone saying that our match-up should have been the state championship game. Earlier in the season, we had squeaked out a win against them, beating Shawnee Mission North 9-8 on our home field. It was one of the closest, hardest-fought games of the season, and now we were about to face them again in the playoffs, this time on their home turf.

The first district playoff game was at Shawnee Mission Northwest's stadium, and the atmosphere was electric. The stands were packed, and the tension was thick in the air. As the game went on, it was a back-and-forth battle, with both teams giving everything they had. We found ourselves tied at 7-7, and the pressure was mounting.

I'll never forget what happened next. My good friend Jan Demby and I were back to return a punt on a crucial fourth down. All season long, Jan and I had a

Chapter Four

little friendly competition—always trying to outdo each other, trying to be the ball hog, the one to make the big play. This time was no different. As the ball came toward us, both of us hesitated, waiting for the other to grab it. The ball hit the ground right between us, and instead of bouncing in our favor, it rolled all the way to our four-yard line. I looked at Jan, he looked at me, and there we were—stuck deep in our own territory with our backs against the wall.

Richard Allen, our punter, had been solid all season, averaging 40 to 45 yards per punt, but on that night, everything seemed to go wrong. We went three downs and out, forced to punt from deep in our end zone. Richard lined up, and as soon as the ball was snapped, disaster struck. The punt came off his foot awkwardly—a shank. It barely went anywhere, and Shawnee Mission Northwest ended up with the ball on our 21-yard line, poised to take the lead.

With time winding down, Shawnee Mission Northwest set up for a field goal. Tony Cisco, their kicker, stepped onto the field, and the stadium held its breath. The kick went up, and it sailed right through the uprights. Shawnee Mission Northwest had just taken a 10-7 lead, and with that, my high school football career was over.

I remember standing there on the field, looking up at the scoreboard, feeling the weight of the loss sink in. We had gone 9-1 that season, won the Sunflower League Championship, and I had even earned All-Sunflower honors as a wide receiver flanker, with an honorable mention. But at that moment, it felt like it had all come to an abrupt end. I wasn't sure what the future held for me.

I remember standing there on the field, looking up at the scoreboard, feeling the weight of the loss sink in. The numbers glowed harshly against the night sky, a reminder that our season—our dream—had just been ripped away. The cold autumn air bit at my skin, but it couldn't match the chill in my chest. We had gone **9-1**, won the **Sunflower League Championship**, and I had earned **All-Sunflower honors** as a **flanker** with an **honorable mention**. But at that moment, none of it seemed to matter.

The field, where we had celebrated so many victories, now felt like unfamiliar ground. The cheers that had followed us all season were gone, replaced by an eerie silence. I could hear the murmurs of teammates, some still in disbelief, others holding back frustration. A few coaches tried to speak, but their voices were lost in the moment.

I saw teammates kneeling in exhaustion, helmets still in hand, staring at the grass as if searching for an answer. Others stood in small groups, shaking their heads, whispering about what went wrong. Someone slammed their helmet to the ground, the sound echoing in the emptying stadium.

"We should've had this."
"Man, this ain't how it was supposed to end."
"I don't even know what to say."

Coach gathered us near the sideline, his voice steady but heavy. **"Hold your heads up. This one hurts, I know. But don't let this loss define what you accomplished this season."** He paused, scanning the faces of a team that had given everything. **"You fought. You battled. And that's**

Chapter Four

something no scoreboard can take away."

Walking off the field was the hardest part. The fans who had supported us all year stood silently, some offering nods of respect, others shaking their heads, just as stunned as we were. The walk to the locker room felt longer than ever. Every step carried the weight of what-ifs and almosts.

Inside, the energy was different. The usual postgame chaos was gone—no laughter, no music, just the sound of cleats scraping against the concrete floor. Some guys sat quietly at their lockers, untying their cleats in slow, deliberate motions. A few still had their heads buried in their hands.

"Man… I just don't get it," someone muttered.
"We were supposed to go all the way."
"This doesn't even feel real."

Coach spoke again, his voice softer now. **"It's okay to feel this. It's okay to be hurt. But don't let it keep you down. This game, this season—it meant something. You're walking out of here as champions of this league. That doesn't change."**

But at that moment, it was hard to believe. The silence stretched on as we sat there, staring at the lockers, at the jerseys, at the empty space where the next game should have been.

I leaned back, staring at the ceiling, my mind racing. I wasn't sure what the future held for me. Football had been everything. But now? Now, I wasn't sure if this was the end of something… or just the beginning of something new.

Then, a glimmer of hope came. I began to receive scholarship offers, and one in particular stood out—Independence Community College in Independence, Kansas. I'll never forget the feeling when Coach Shonka called me and offered me a chance to play for Independence. I took a visit to the campus, and immediately, I knew it was the right place for me. Coach Shonka believed in my abilities and saw me as a key player in his offense. Without hesitation, I signed to play as a flanker for Independence Community College.

That decision opened up the next chapter of my life. Though my time at Lawrence High had come to an end, I wanted to hold onto my relationships for as long as possible.

To keep my love for sports alive and not feel the brunt too strongly for how my life would change, I played baseball that summer with all the familiar faces. I had an exceptional season playing for the Breakfast Optimists, and man, we had a great team. It was great to feel that chemistry one last time as talented high school athletes. I still remember the lineup of players who made every game feel like something special: Carl Boldra, Frank Easum, Rob Steer, John Byers, Frank Heck, Kenny Romero, Darren Cole—just to name a few. Then there were guys like David Johnson in the outfield, Stephen Scott, and Mike and Chris Bennett, who always brought their best to the field.

I had an exceptional season playing for the Breakfast Optimists, and looking back, it was more than just a team—it was a collection of raw talent, chemistry, and heart. That season was special, not just because of the games we won, but because of the way we played to-

Chapter Four

gether, pushed each other, and elevated every moment on the field. We had something rare—a team where every player brought something unique, a combination of skill, grit, and passion that made every game feel like an event.

I still remember that lineup—guys who weren't just good, they were game-changers. Carl Boldra had the kind of natural leadership and instinct that made him a cornerstone of the team. Frank Easum, smooth and effortless in his execution, a quiet force who always came through when it mattered. Rob Steer had the kind of presence that demanded attention, his confidence and control setting the tone. John Byers was as reliable as they came—fundamentally sound and always in the right place at the right time.

Then there was Frank Heck, a player with an undeniable fire in his belly, the kind of competitor you wanted in the clutch. Kenny Romero—explosive, athletic, and unpredictable in the best way. Darren Cole brought an edge, that spark that could ignite the team in a heartbeat. And in the outfield, David Johnson covered ground like he had wings, tracking down fly balls that seemed destined to drop.

Stephen Scott had a work ethic that set him apart, a guy you could always count on to give 100%. And then there was Mike and Chris—two players who played with heart and instinct, always dialed in, always finding ways to contribute.

That team was more than just a collection of good players. We understood each other. We trusted each other. Every game was a reminder of what made us special—talent, yes, but also the unspoken connection

Making a Name for Myself

that made us more than just teammates. It was great to feel that chemistry one last time as high school athletes, to leave it all on the field with a group of guys who made every moment count.

It wasn't just a season. It was a legacy. And it's one I'll never forget.

That year, we were a force to be reckoned with, finishing the season with a remarkable 36-11 record. Playing for the Breakfast Optimists was a thrill, especially with Coach Bob Rogers at the helm, guiding us through a season full of unforgettable moments. One game that still stands out was when we played against the Eudora team.

Carl Boldra, always one to shine, went five-for-five that day, and we ended up beating them 10-7. I remember it like it was yesterday. The game was tied at 8-8 late in the innings, tension mounting with every pitch. There I was, standing at the plate with a chance to make a difference. What did I do? I laid down a suicide squeeze bunt, and David Johnson charged home from third base, scoring the winning run. That feeling of excitement, knowing you played a part in your team's success, is something I'll never forget. On top of that, it was the same game where I hit my first home run of the season, which was the cherry on top.

Later that same week, we swept De Soto in the Babe Ruth tournament, continuing our hot streak. My buddy Frank Heck went three-for-four in one of those games, and Stephen Scott slugged two solid doubles. Rob Steer, always reliable on the mound, pitched a complete game to secure another victory for us. I had a pretty

Chapter Four

good game myself, with a double and a triple, helping to keep our momentum rolling.

One of our biggest challenges came later in the season when we played KC Security, a tough team that always brought out the best in us. Rob Steer pitched yet another complete game, and I had a standout performance, going four-for-four with two doubles and a triple. Those kinds of games reminded me just how much I loved being a part of this team.

Of course, I can't forget our rivalry with the Baldwin baseball club. They always gave us a run for our money, but that Friday night in the Eudora tournament was a different story. The Breakfast Optimists made short work of Baldwin, beating them 14-2 in a game that was called after the third inning due to the 10-run rule. They made several errors in the first inning, and we took full advantage, jumping out to a huge lead that they could never overcome.

As my coach, Roger Terry, would often say, "Baldwin made some costly mistakes," and he was right. Baldwin committed seven errors in that game against the Breakfast Optimists, most of them coming in the very first inning. We capitalized on those mistakes and put up three runs right away. By the second inning, we were unstoppable, exploding for eight runs. Mike Bennett was in complete control on the mound, allowing only four hits, all singles, and no extra-base hits.

The very next day, during the tournament, Frank Easum put on a show. He shut down the KC Elliott team with a two-hit pitching performance. Not only that, but Frank helped his own cause with a first-inning grand slam that set the tone for the rest of the game. We won 15-3, and once again, the game was called early due to the 10-run rule. I remember that day vividly—I walked once, struck out once, but still went four-for-four at the plate. I handed the ball off to Mike Bennett after my solid start, and he took care of business, keeping us in control the entire game.

Frank Heck also had a big night, going three-for-three with two doubles. I went two-for-two with two walks, scoring three runs and adding two RBIs. That game really highlighted what a special team we had. We weren't just skilled players—we were a tight-knit group with incredible chemistry that showed on the field, and Coach Rogers knew how to bring the best out of us.

Later in the season, we faced off against the Topeka Cotton Belt team in a much-anticipated opener. It was another showcase of our strength. John Byrns, Mike Bennett, David Johnson, and I each had two hits, and all of us got on base. Vance Kempin led the charge from the mound, pitching a gem and guiding us to an 8-1 victory. That win set the tone for the rest of the season, and Coach Rogers was thrilled. He reminded us how important it was to keep building momentum. Thankfully, we managed to complete that game just before a rainstorm hit, adding a little extra drama to an already exciting night.

One of the standout moments from that season was when we traveled down to Gardner. By then, the Breakfast Optimists were well on their way to making a deep run in the state playoffs, and Gardner was just another step on our journey. We dominated the first game, winning 14-2, and I kicked things off by leading off with a

Chapter Four

home run. That shot was one of those moments where you just feel locked in—it felt like the ball would sail forever. The energy from that home run carried through the game, and we kept piling on runs.

The second game against Gardner was more of the same. We won 14-8, and everyone on the team contributed in some way. Those back-to-back wins were a testament to our resilience and determination. It wasn't just about having talented players—it was about showing up every game, working as a unit, and executing the fundamentals. Those moments playing for the Breakfast Optimists were some of the best in my life. We had an outstanding team, a great coach in Bob Rogers, and a bond that made us feel unbeatable.

As the season marched on and we prepared for the state playoffs, we were confident and focused, knowing we had the potential to go all the way. It wasn't just the victories that made it special; it was the friendships, the lessons, and the memories we created together on and off the field. Each game, each win, brought us closer, and those summers with the Breakfast Optimists became a defining part of my athletic journey.

That summer was filled with moments like these—moments that shaped me as a competitor and teammate. Every game, every at-bat, every play on the field contributed to a season that would forever be etched in my memory. It was the kind of summer that made me feel invincible, ready to take on whatever came next.

Leaving Lawrence to play baseball at Highland Community College marked a pivotal moment in my journey. After a solid high school career, I initially signed to play football at Independence Community College.. But my passion for baseball led me to focus solely on the sport, which eventually brought me to Highland. I had envisioned my college career taking off from there, but life had different plans. I couldn't ignore the growing problems I was facing off the field—addiction to drugs and alcohol.

STEVE BARBEE
RETURN SPECIALTIES
ALL AMERICAN
1984

S. Barbee makes one of his winning catches for the S...tion

Chapter FIVE

FIRST STEPS INTO ADDICTION: COLLEGE GLORY

The contrast between my upbringing and my struggle with substance abuse is stark. I grew up in a household where family was central, and drugs or alcohol had no place. But when I stepped out of that environment, the streets and peer pressure introduced me to a different world. It started small—weekend keg parties, smoking marijuana, drinking beer at local hangouts—but that recreational use began to escalate when I got to college.

My addiction affected more than my personal life—it cost me my baseball scholarship. With my GPA dropping to 1.47, I was declared ineligible for the spring 1983 season. The weight of that failure was heavy, and I remember feeling both ashamed and lost. The scholar-

Chapter Five

ship had been my ticket to fulfilling a childhood dream, and now that dream was slipping away because of my own choices.

Trying to salvage what I could, I stayed in shape by going out for spring football, but the loss of my scholarship stung deeply. I came home that winter, desperately trying to justify my situation. I even picked up the phone and called other schools that had previously recruited me for baseball, telling them that Highland wasn't the right fit. But deep down, I knew I was only running from the consequences of my actions.

Then came a moment that changed everything—my father called me upstairs. He didn't sugarcoat it. He simply said, "No, son. You're going back to Highland. You'll face your teammates, classmates, and everyone you let down." That conversation cut through my excuses. It was humbling and painful, but it was a necessary turning point in my life. I knew then that I had to confront the reality of my choices.

Then came the second wave. "It's a girl." And just like that, the ground beneath me shifted. A daughter. My daughter. Latasha Marie. Born September 9, 1983.

I remember the name echoing in my head like a bell tolling in a cathedral. Holy. Final. Unavoidable. She wasn't just a baby she was my baby. A living, breathing extension of me. And not only that, she was the first grandchild in the Barbee family the first of a new generation.

That realization didn't just stir something in me it wrecked me. I hadn't been there for her birth. I hadn't

First Steps Into Addiction: College Glory

held her tiny fingers or kissed her forehead. I hadn't prayed over her crib or whispered promises like a father should. I didn't know how to be present because I didn't know how to be still. Football gave me plays, purpose, and praise but this? This was uncharted territory.

This was legacy. This was fatherhood. And I was scared to death. There was no coach calling the next play. No whistle to reset the down. Just me, standing on the edge of something sacred and terrifying, with no idea how to take the first step. And as the reality of her birth began to settle in, another weight pressed against my chest like a cinder block: I had to tell my parents.

This wasn't just a conversation it felt like a confession. A fall from grace. My parents were pillars of faith. My father, a devoted pastor. My mother, a quiet warrior of wisdom and prayer. We were raised on truth, shaped by Scripture, and disciplined in love. The Bible wasn't a book in our house—it was the foundation. So how could I look them in the eye and say that their son—the athlete, the one they bragged about at church had fathered a child outside of wedlock?

The shame sat in my gut like stone. Heavy. Unmovable. I played the moment in my head a hundred times how they would look at me, what they might say. I didn't fear anger. What I feared was their disappointment. That look from my mother that pierced deeper than any shout. That silence from my father that carried more weight than a sermon. They had invested so much in me. Prayed over me. Believed in me.

And now, their first grandchild would be born in a way they never hoped or planned for. But there was no

Chapter Five

hiding from this. No spin, no excuse. I had to own it—not just as a mistake, but as a man stepping into responsibility. And whether their hearts broke or not, I had to trust that somewhere, beneath the grief, there would still be grace.

I also feared what this would do to my identity. What would people say back home? What would the church community whisper? "That's Pastor Barbee's son the one who had a baby out of wedlock." What would it do to my future, my reputation, my image?

But even then, I could sense that God was already at work. Teaching me that healing can't come without honesty. That exposure is the beginning of transformation. That freedom only comes through the truth.

So with trembling hands and a soul full of uncertainty, I prepared to speak the words that would alter everything:

"Her name is Latasha Marie. She was born on September 9th. She's my daughter." I didn't know how my parents would respond. But I knew this I wasn't running from it anymore.

Not from the truth.

Not from her.

And not from the man God was calling me to become. But becoming that man didn't happen overnight. The truth is—even after I told my parents... even after I accepted that I had a daughter... I didn't fully step into the role of a father. I wanted to. I told myself I would. But I didn't.

First Steps Into Addiction: College Glory

I was there but not really. I showed up in flashes. A phone call here. A visit there. But it wasn't consistent, and it wasn't enough.

Latasha probably spent more time wondering if she mattered than knowing that she did. And that haunts me. Because the truth is I was chasing my own demons.

Drugs. Alcohol. Women. The streets. The hustle.

All of it had a stronger grip on me than responsibility did. I didn't know how to be a father because I didn't know how to face myself. I was lost in addiction, drowning in guilt, running from accountability. I was selfish. I made choices that prioritized my pain over her peace.

Cocaine numbed the guilt.

Alcohol blurred the shame.

Football and women gave me a temporary high.

But I never stopped long enough to face the man in the mirror. Every time I thought about being a dad, the voice of failure whispered, "You've already blown it." So I pulled back. Disappeared. Reappeared. Disappeared again.

And Latasha... she didn't get a say in any of that. She was just a little girl innocent, blameless, navigating a world of silence, absence, and unanswered

questions.

"Where's my daddy?"

Chapter Five

"Why doesn't he come see me?"

"Does he love me?"

Those aren't just questions they're open wounds. And the weight of them doesn't just live in my memory. It lives in my bones. It took years too many years before I realized that being a father isn't about perfection. It's not about waiting until you've figured everything out. It's about showing up. Even broken. Even scared. Even unsure.

It's about surrendering to God, confronting your shame, and letting grace rebuild what you tore down. I can't rewrite the past. But I can tell the truth.

I was in and out of her life because I was lost.

Lost in addiction.

Lost in guilt.

Lost in selfishness.

But I thank God—over and over again—that He never gave up on me. That He's still writing the story between a father and his daughter.

And that every time I say her name Latasha Marie it's not just a reminder of what I missed... It's a promise of what I still hope to restore.

During the spring and fall of 1983, I was determined to bounce back. My grades had slipped before, but I worked hard to pull them up, and by the time football season rolled around, I had managed to boost my GPA

First Steps Into Addiction: College Glory

to a solid 3.2, making me eligible to play again. Football was my second chance, and I didn't want to waste it. The combination of football and my personal redemption off the field made 1983 a year of both struggle and triumph. I realized that while my battle with addiction had cost me my baseball scholarship, I still had a chance to rewrite my story on the football field.

The 1983 football season had a mix of high expectations and uncertainty. The season opener, on September 10th, took us to Crete, Nebraska, to face the Doane College Tigers JV. It was a tough game, with us trailing 17-0 by halftime. But in the second half, Coach Allen opened up the offense, and we started to fight back.

One of the key moments came when Marion Kelly recovered a fumble deep in Tiger territory. Freshman quarterback Carl Boldra took the helm, and after two quick plays, he threw a 23-yard pass to me, setting us up on the six-yard line. Although we lost some yards on the next play, Boldra hit Randy Davis in the end zone for our first touchdown. Chris Schwartz added the extra point, and we were back in the game.

Later, with just 4:27 left in the fourth quarter, down 19-7, Boldra started driving us down the field. He connected with me twice for a total of 28 yards, then found Kenny Kellum wide-open for a 30-yard gain. I caught another pass for 14 yards to bring us to Doane's 16-yard line, but after a few incompletions, Boldra hit Steve Harshaw, who spun into the end zone for a score. We were now only five points behind, but despite our best efforts—including an onside kick—we couldn't get the ball back. Nevertheless, our defense held Doane scoreless in the second half, and we showed real grit.

Chapter Five

Our offense that day was explosive, racking up 372 total yards, 240 of them through the air. I hauled in five catches for 74 yards, while Randy Davis and Steve Harshaw both had key receptions. Though the loss stung, it showed we had the potential to compete with anyone.

The following week, on September 17th, we faced Haskell Indian Junior College. This time, we were determined to avoid a slow start. Unfortunately, Haskell jumped ahead early, with an 8-0 lead thanks to an interception and a safety. But we kept our composure. Late in the first quarter, I returned a punt 21 yards to Haskell's 31-yard line, giving our offense a spark. Greg Brown took over from there, running it in for a 24-yard touchdown. Chris Schwartz nailed the extra point, and we were right back in it.

In that game, we dominated Haskell, ultimately winning 34-14. Our defense was relentless, holding Haskell to only one more score late in the fourth quarter. On offense, we found our rhythm, and it felt good to be part of a team that was starting to click. I contributed on special teams and helped set up key plays, and with each game, my confidence in my new position grew.

brokeAs the clock ticked down in the first half, we knew we needed to score before halftime. The atmosphere on the field was tense but charged with determination. Highland's offense, which had been steadily building momentum, took over at our 25-yard line with just over five minutes to play before the break. The pressure was on, but so was our focus.

On the first play, Carl Boldra, our quarterback, dropped back and fired a dart to Kenny Kellum, who

First Steps Into Addiction: College Glory

sprinted down the sideline for a 21-yard gain. The crowd roared, sensing that something big was about to unfold. Without hesitation, Boldra hit Steve Harshaw on the next play, threading the ball between defenders for another 14 yards. You could feel the Haskell defense getting nervous, unsure whether to expect another pass or a run.

Keeping them guessing, Boldra handed the ball off to our bruising fullback, Scott Williams. Williams barreled through the line, dragging defenders with him for a tough six-yard gain, pushing us into Haskell territory at the 34-yard line. The energy on the sideline was electric; we could smell the end zone.

Then it was my turn. Boldra called my number, and I ran a clean route, cutting across the middle of the field. The ball sailed toward me, and I snatched it out of the air for an eight-yard pickup, another crucial first down. The Haskell defense was on its heels, scrambling to adjust as we methodically moved the ball. At this point, we were 12 yards from the goal line, and everyone could feel we were about to punch it in.

With precision and calm, Boldra took the snap, scanned the field, and lofted a perfect pass to Randy Davis, who had slipped past his defender in the corner of the end zone. The ball seemed to hang in the air for a moment before Davis reeled it in, his feet tapping down just inside the sideline for the touchdown. The sideline erupted in cheers as Chris Schwartz trotted out and nailed the extra point, giving us a 14-8 lead as we headed into halftime.

Coach Allen's halftime talk was short and to the point: we had the momentum, but we couldn't let up. The

Chapter Five

second half was ours for the taking, and we had to seize it. We came out of the locker room hungry, fired up, and ready to put the game out of reach.

Haskell's first possession of the second half ended quickly, as Kevin Williams intercepted a pass at our 24-yard line, shifting the game's momentum even further in our favor. Ron Smith, back at quarterback, wasted no time. On the very next play, he found Harshaw with an 11-yard pass that kept the defense honest. Then, on the following play, Smith unleashed a perfectly placed 35-yard bomb to Harshaw again. He outran the Haskell secondary and raced into the end zone. Though the extra point attempt failed, we had extended our lead to 22-8.

Early in the fourth quarter, we struck again. This time, it was a beautiful passing play that stretched the field. Smith, calm and collected in the pocket, hit Randy Davis on a crossing pattern. Davis turned upfield and blazed past defenders, sprinting 35 yards untouched for another touchdown. The drive covered 69 yards in just a few plays, and Schwartz's extra point gave us a commanding 27-8 lead.

Haskell, to their credit, didn't fold. They mounted a 65-yard scoring drive late in the game, narrowing the gap to 27-14, but when they went for a two-point conversion, Wayne Deed dashed their hopes with a perfectly timed interception. Just when it seemed like Haskell might have one last chance to score, our defense came up big again. John Paul, a standout freshman, made the play of the game, intercepting a pass at the 30-yard line and rumbling all the way back for a touchdown. Schwartz added the extra point, sealing our 34-14 victory. It was a resounding statement—our first win of the season, and we had earned it.

Coach Allen was beaming after the game. He praised our second-half performance, particularly the defense, which had completely shut down Haskell after the early hiccups. The victory was exactly what we needed to build confidence for the season ahead. Next week, we'd face the Washburn JV team, and we were ready.

However, when September 26th rolled around, things didn't go as planned. We traveled to Topeka to take on Washburn's junior varsity, and from the outset, we knew it would be a tough game. Washburn jumped out to an early lead, and although we fought hard, we struggled to find consistency.

Our defense kept us in the game, bottling up Washburn's running attack and recording several key sacks. Linebackers Tom Kelsey and Scott Albin were all over the field, while Roger Brown, Jerry Cartwright, and Kevin Peterson also put constant pressure on their quarterback. Marion Kelly, Wayne Deed, and Jeff Williams each snatched interceptions, with Williams nearly taking one back to the house, returning it to the one-yard line to set up a touchdown.

Despite the defense's heroics, our offense couldn't get going in the first half. We missed a field goal and fumbled the ball at the one-yard line, squandering golden opportunities. Washburn took advantage, building a 28-6 lead early in the fourth quarter. It looked like we were done for, but Highland didn't quit.

With 9:55 left in the game, Carl Boldra started to find his rhythm. He connected with me for a 19-yard

Chapter Five

gain, giving us a first down at Washburn's 45-yard line. After a couple of incompletions, Reggie Johnson powered through for a seven-yard run, bringing us to a critical fourth down. We were still down, but we refused to give up. The game wasn't over until the final whistle, and we were determined to keep fighting.

In one of the most thrilling football performances at Highland Community College, the Scotties fought hard against Washburn, showing their tenacity despite the game's challenges. A penalty pushed the team back five yards, forcing them to punt. However, in a bold move, the punter swept right from the punt formation and managed to gain 12 yards, keeping the drive alive. Highland was in scoring position again, and two plays later, quarterback Carl Boldra connected with Kenny Calvin for a 31-yard touchdown pass. Though the two-point conversion attempt failed, narrowing the gap to 28-12, the Scotties were back in the game.

Highland's defense stepped up when Jeff Williamsay made a crucial interception, returning the ball to Washburn's 1-yard line. Just four plays later, Greg Brown broke through the defense on a sweep to the right side, scoring for Highland. Boldra then found Randy Davis for a successful two-point conversion, bringing the score to 28-20 with seven minutes remaining. Highland managed to get the ball back but couldn't mount another scoring drive, ultimately falling short in a valiant effort. The Scotties prepared for their next game, set for October 3, 1983, where they would travel to Blair, Nebraska, to face Dana College.

This game marked a pivotal moment for me as the team sought a new tailback. The star running back, Kev-

First Steps Into Addiction: College Glory

in Long, had suffered a season-ending knee injury, and Kevin Brown, who had taken over as first-team running back, struggled to fill the void. I remember vividly the conversation Coach Marty Allen and I had.

"Barbee, didn't you play running back at Lawrence High School?" Coach Allen asked, with his trademark smile and cigar in hand. I affirmed that I had, and Coach Allen made me an offer: "We need a better running back, and I guarantee you'll carry the ball 18 to 20 times a game."

This was my chance for me to accept the challenge of moving from wide receiver to tailback. In his first game at his new position, Barbee made an immediate impact, scoring three touchdowns in a commanding 50-30 victory over Dana College. He exploded with runs of 60, 69, and 14 yards, breaking the Highland rushing record with a staggering 278 yards on 29 carries. His performance reinvigorated the team, pushing them to a 2-2 record. John Paul also contributed to the win with a 30-yard interception return for a touchdown, while Chris Swartz nailed the extra points to solidify the Scotties' victory.

One week later, on October 10, 1983, the Scotties traveled to Tarkio, Missouri, to face the Owls. Highland dominated from the start, scoring three first-half touchdowns to take a 21-0 lead by halftime. The first score came on a beautifully executed 25-yard pass from Ron Smith to Kenny Keller, who made a spectacular diving catch in the end zone. Chris Swartz's extra point made it 7-0.

With just over five minutes left in the half, I took

Chapter Five

the spotlight again, sprinting 17 yards around the left end for another Highland score. Swartz's conversion made it 14-0. Minutes later, Carl Boldra threw a seven-yard touchdown pass to Keller, with Swartz converting again to send the Scotties into halftime up 21-0.

Our write-up on the college campus read something like, "In the second half, Highland wasted no time extending their lead. Just 39 seconds in, I broke free for a 55-yard touchdown run, all but sealing the fate of the Owls. Although Tarkio managed two late touchdowns, they couldn't keep up with the Scotties' dominant performance. The Highland defense held the Owls to just 226 yards of total offense and forced three interceptions—two by standout defender John Paul Twombly and one returned by Wayne Dieter. Swartz closed out the game with two field goals, from 27 and 37 yards, as the Scotties rolled to a decisive 34-14 win.

The victory over Tarkio not only elevated Highland's record but also showcased the team's offensive prowess, racking up 393 total yards, while the defense held firm against any attempts at a comeback. My leadership and record-setting performance at tailback solidified my place as a key player for the Scotties, marking the beginning of an impressive run for Highland Community College."

On Monday night, October 17, 1983, we faced the Benedictine Ravens' junior varsity team at Kissinger Field in Highland, Kansas. The Scotties' offense proved to be their own worst enemy, as they turned the ball over seven times in a tough 33-24 loss. Despite the high-scoring game, the defense kept Highland in the contest, showcasing an outstanding effort that the offense could not fully capitalize on.

Coach Marty Allen's post-game comments summed it up: "You can't make the mistakes we did and give them the opportunities we did. The defense, despite the 33 points scored against them, was as good as it has been all year." Highland's defensive stars that night included linebacker Tom Kelsey of Oak Grove, Missouri, and Scott Albin from Nebraska, who played key roles in keeping the game within reach. Another defensive standout, Mike Krantz from Wedmore, Kansas, made a crucial interception deep in Highland territory, stopping one of the Ravens' scoring drives.

The offensive side of the ball had its moments, though consistency was a struggle. The offensive line managed to open up some holes for me, as I rushed for 146 yards on 27 carries, but there were also key breakdowns in protecting quarterback Ron Smith. Despite these challenges, the Scotties kept the game close. Trailing 17-14, we pulled off a remarkable play when Carl Boldra, the holder on a fake field goal attempt, rolled out to his right and hit Randy Davis for a 27-yard touchdown pass, briefly giving the Scotties the lead in the second half.

Chris Swartz then kicked a 22-yard field goal to narrow the gap to 23-17 in the third quarter. The momentum shifted again as I powered in a two-yard touchdown run to put Highland ahead. However, the Ravens came right back with a field goal, retaking the lead at 26-24 with just over five minutes remaining.

Tragedy struck late in the game when I went down with an ankle injury while returning a kickoff, forcing

Chapter Five

me to sit out the rest of the contest. The Scotties fought hard, advancing to the Ravens' 35-yard line, but they ran out of downs. On their final drive, an interception returned for a touchdown sealed Highland's fate, dropping our record to 3-3.

One week later, on October 24, 1983, Highland faced Northwest Missouri State's junior varsity squad at Kissinger Field. The Scotties rebounded from the previous week's disappointment with a dominant 34-16 win, showcasing a powerful second-half surge. The game remained close in the first half, but Highland exploded for 29 points in the second half, cruising to victory.

The defense was once again instrumental in the win. After the game, Coach Allen praised the defense: "The defense came out, got the interception, and really turned the game around. They gave the Scotties the momentum we needed." Highland never trailed, but the game was tight until the third quarter when the Scotties broke it open.

The turning point came when Mark Jackman recovered a fumble, setting up Highland on the Bearcats' 46-yard line. Boldra completed three passes for 36 yards, moving the ball to the 6-yard line. From there, I punched it in for the score, with Swartz adding the extra point to make it 7-0.

Northwest Missouri State managed to drive down the field and score just before halftime, but a missed two-point conversion left the score at 7-6 in favor of the Scotties. The second half began with Highland in control. I returned a punt from our 35-yard line, thanks to a key block by Scott Albin, sprinting 65 yards for a touchdown.

First Steps Into Addiction: College Glory

The momentum continued to swing in Highland's favor when Marion Kelly, from Atchison, Kansas, intercepted a pass and returned it to the Bearcats' 10-yard line. Although the offense couldn't punch it in, Swartz converted a 23-yard field goal to extend the lead to 16-6. The defense continued to shine.

Chris Ostrich sacked the Bearcats' quarterback, forcing a punt and giving the Scotties prime field position deep in Bearcat territory. On the very next play, I once again made my presence felt, cutting through the defense for another touchdown as Highland's lead ballooned to 23-6. With the defense holding strong and the offense clicking, the Scotties added two more scores in the final quarter, including another field goal from Swartz and a defensive touchdown after a fumble recovery. By the end of the game, the Highland Scotties had accumulated 393 yards while holding the Bearcats to just 226 yards.

This emphatic victory over Northwest Missouri State's junior varsity team moved the Scotties to a 4-3 record, leaving us with plenty of momentum as we prepared for their next challenge. My dynamic play on both offense and special teams, coupled with the defense's relentless pressure, signaled that the Scotties were hitting their stride as the season progressed.

Chapter Five

Chapter SIX

THE STAKES KEPT RISING

The fall of 1983 was supposed to be about football. The grind of two-a-days, the raw anticipation before kickoff, the bruises that didn't hurt nearly as much as the thought of being overlooked. It was about the Saturday night lights, the roar of the crowd when I broke a tackle, the adrenaline rush of chasing records and recognition. I was locked in at least on the surface. Hungry for greatness. Determined to escape everything I had seen growing up. Football made sense. It gave me structure. Identity. Even glory.

But no amount of touchdowns could've prepared me for the news that would blindside me harder than any linebacker ever could. I was going to be a father. Those words didn't register at first. They hit the surface of my mind and bounced off like they belonged to someone else's story. I stood still in the echo of it caught between disbelief and panic, between a rising fear and a hollow numbness that settled deep in my gut. I was just a kid

Chapter Six

myself, still trying to figure out who I was, still trying to prove something to the world. How could I be a father when I was barely holding together the fractured pieces of a young man chasing approval?

In one of the most exhilarating moments of the 1983 season, I scored my third touchdown of the game, sweeping around the left side with precision. I cut through the defense, eluding would-be tacklers, and bolted into the end zone, adding another highlight to the night. But the action didn't stop there. It was time for Tom Kelsey to step into the spotlight, and he did so in dramatic fashion, intercepting a pass and racing it back to the 10-yard line. The crowd roared as he set up yet another scoring opportunity.

Quarterback Carl Boldra, poised under pressure, threw a strike over the middle to Kenny Kellum. On the very next play, I pitched the ball to Leo Ballard, who barreled into the end zone for the final touchdown of the game, sealing a decisive victory. The win lifted our record to 4-3, and we were riding high with momentum heading into the next matchup against Missouri Western State College at Kissinger Field.

Of all the games that season, one of the most memorable was our clash with Kansas State University's junior varsity team in Manhattan, Kansas. It was an intense battle, and I'll never forget the thrill of that game. We struck first, taking the lead with a dazzling 78-yard touchdown run. I remember the play vividly: the offensive line opened a perfect lane, and I sprinted down the field, outpacing the Wildcats' defense. The roar of the crowd filled the air as I crossed into the end zone, and Chris Swartz's extra point made it 7-0 in favor of the Scotties.

However, the Kansas State JV, determined and relentless, stormed back. Carlos Adams tied the game with a strong run, and the Wildcats added to their lead in the third quarter with a 28-yard touchdown pass from their quarterback to Hannah. The turning point came when Adams broke away for an 82-yard run that left us trailing 19-7. Still, we didn't give up. Robbie Golder caught a five-yard touchdown pass from Ron Smith, and Swartz's extra point brought us within striking distance at 19-14.

But K-State's offense continued to press. Grossman took off on a 75-yard run, pushing their lead to 28-14, and they capped it off with a 38-yard field goal. Despite our best efforts, we couldn't close the gap, and the Wildcats walked away with the 28-14 victory. For me, that game was both a personal and team milestone. I had 29 carries for 102 yards, a testament to my endurance and determination. Even though we came up short, the experience was unforgettable.

The 1983 season, as a whole, was a breakout year for me. I finished the season with 119 carries, racking up 840 yards. My longest run that year was a 77-yard sprint, and I averaged an impressive 7.5 yards per carry. I was also a key player in the passing game, catching 24 passes for 212 yards, with my longest reception being 23 yards. I scored a total of 10 touchdowns, contributing 60 points to the team's success.

Reflecting on that year, I take great pride in my role as an all-purpose running back. Whether it was rushing, receiving, or contributing on special teams, I was able to make an impact on the field. It was a season filled with highs and lows, but one that cemented my love for the game and my place as a key contributor for Highland

Chapter Six

Community College.

In the 1983 football season, I put up some of my best performances as a running back and return specialist at Highland Community College. On punt returns, I had 15 for 285 yards, and one of those electrifying returns went for a touchdown. With an average of 19 yards per punt return, I made sure every opportunity counted. On kickoff returns, I added 258 more yards, rounding off my return game to make a real impact on special teams.

By the end of the season, I had rushed for 840 yards on 119 carries, ranking me 7th in Highland's all-time individual top seasons and 11th in carries for a season. I led Highland in rushing, finishing 14th in the nation with 840 yards. I was also ranked as the nation's top all-purpose yardage leader with 1,488 yards.

My ability to contribute through the air also showed, with 24 receptions, earning me the 8th spot in Highland's all-time individual records. Some of my career highlights included a 78-yard run against Kansas State and a 69-yard dash against Dana College, ranking me among Highland's top performers. I even held the record for 3rd most kickoff return yards in Highland history with 251 yards.

I was fortunate to receive several awards that year, including Best Offensive Back and MVP on offense. This season didn't just show me what I could do on the field, but it also built my confidence, proving that my determination could lead me to success in all areas of life.

The 1984 season kicked off with explosive energy when we faced Doane College of Nebraska. Right from

The Stakes Kept Rising

the start, I was on fire, powering my way to two first-half touchdowns with relentless drives of 4 and 15 yards, helping Highland Community College to a 32-6 rout.

My brother Jeff chipped in with a two-yard score as we stormed to a 23-0 lead by halftime. Jerry Cartwright also added to the early domination with a sack for a safety, and Dennis McGovern punched in a four-yard TD in the third quarter to stretch our lead even further. Doane's only answer came late, with a 25-yard pass, but by then, the game was long over.

For me, it was a solid start: 13 carries for 65 yards, two touchdowns, seven punt returns totaling 52 yards, and a 20-yard kickoff return. We were locked in, and it showed in every phase of the game. The team up next was Tarkio College, and we rolled over them, winning 33-8. That game, played in front of our home crowd in Highland, was a dominant performance from start to finish.

We surged to a 21-0 halftime lead, with the Owls managing a late score when the game was well in hand. I was locked into my rhythm, finishing with 138 yards on 24 carries and three touchdowns. Coach Marty Allen couldn't say enough about the offensive line's performance that day, crediting them for opening up huge lanes that made my job easier. He felt we played an even better offensive game than our opener.

But it wasn't just me—Jeff had a great game, too, with six carries for 62 yards, while our quarterbacks, Carl Boldra and Dennis McGovern, connected on 7 of 23 passes for 132 yards and a touchdown. Jan Demby, a reliable target from Lawrence, Kansas, caught two passes

Chapter Six

for 83 yards, including a spectacular 48-yard touchdown.

On defense, we were just as fierce, holding the Owls to a meager 62 yards rushing and 105 yards through the air. Chris Ebert had an outstanding day, grabbing two interceptions, including a 48-yard return for a touchdown. Coach Allen was thrilled with the defense's dominance, noting how they outdid their already stellar performance from the Doane game.

Our third game, against MidAmerica Nazarene, saw us continue our winning ways with a 31-12 victory. Carl Boldra threw three touchdown passes, two of which came my way, giving us the momentum to remain undefeated.

That season wasn't just about stats and scores; it was about finding another gear on the field and showing what we could achieve as a team, driven by discipline, teamwork, and a relentless desire to win. Each game was a chance to showcase my abilities, and I took that opportunity to prove myself again and again.

The 1984 season was one of those years where every game seemed to build on the last, and the action never let up. After starting the season strong, we entered our third game against MidAmerica Nazarene, riding high. In that game, I scored two touchdowns, both on precision passes from Carl Boldra. The first touchdown came on a 29-yard strike, hitting me with 11:57 left in the first quarter. The connection was flawless as we began to build momentum early on. Carl found me again later in the quarter for another touchdown, this time on a well-executed 10-yard pass with just 20 seconds left on the clock. We were clicking on all cylinders.

The Stakes Kept Rising

We kept the pressure on with Greg Ashworth adding a 27-yard field goal, followed by a 37-yard pass from me to my close friend Jan Demby in the second quarter. It was one of those special plays where everything aligned perfectly. Ashworth also came through with three extra-point conversions, maintaining our lead throughout the game. MidAmerica Nazarene tried to rally with a 65-yard pass from Franklin to Moore in the first quarter, but by then, we had firmly taken control of the game, walking away with a 31-12 victory. That win moved us to a 3-0 record.

Next up, we hosted Bismarck Community College, and once again, we put on a show. We dominated early, scoring 31 points in the first half on the way to a 38-7 victory. Carl Boldra was on fire, throwing two second-quarter touchdown passes, further cementing our undefeated start to the season.

However, our perfect record came to a halt against Missouri Western in a Monday night game. It was a tough one to swallow, as we fell 14-13 in a game decided by inches and small mistakes. Missouri Western's defense got the upper hand early, intercepting us twice. The first interception was returned 23 yards for a touchdown, and just a few minutes later, Tim Gardner punched in a four-yard run for another score. Despite falling behind 14-0 in the first quarter, we battled back hard. I was the leading rusher, putting up 65 yards, and we had a touchdown called back in the third quarter due to a clipping penalty. It was one of those moments where you feel the game slip away.

Still, with just over 10 minutes left in the fourth quarter, Carl Boldra found my brother Jeff for a 16-yard

Chapter Six

touchdown, and Ashworth's extra point brought us within one.

Late in the game, I broke free for a 50-yard run, setting up a crucial two-point conversion attempt. But the decision to go for two proved costly. Missouri Western blocked the kick, and we couldn't convert, sealing our first loss of the season. We dropped to 4-1, knowing we had left some points on the field.

We regrouped quickly and bounced back against Haskell Indian Nations University the following week in Lawrence. It was homecoming for many of us, and we were determined to put on a show for the home crowd at Haskell Stadium. The game turned into a rout, with Highland putting up a 48-0 lead by halftime. I was part of a backfield full of former Lawrence High School players, including Carl Boldra as quarterback, my brother Jeff as a fullback, and Jan Demby as a wide receiver. It was like a reunion, and we were all in sync.

Haskell fought back in the second half, scoring on their first two possessions with Fernando connecting on a touchdown pass to Richard Martinez. But by then, the game was far out of reach. We cruised to a 61-14 victory, improving to 5-1 on the season. Haskell's coach praised our team after the game, saying we deserved our national ranking, and it felt great to prove it in front of the home crowd. Despite their 0-6 record, Haskell showed resilience, and their coach was proud of their effort, especially in the second half.

It was an incredible feeling being part of a team so dominant. That season, each win was more than just a number in the standings—it was a testament to the work

The Stakes Kept Rising

we had put in and the brotherhood we built on the field. From the highs of our big wins to the heartbreak of the close loss, 1984 was a year when we truly left everything on the field.

The Highland Community College Scotties were riding high with a 6-1 record after their victory over Haskell, but their momentum came to a halt on Monday, October 18th, when they faced the University of Nebraska Omaha Mavericks JV. It was a game where the first half seemed promising, but the second half turned into a nightmare. We came out strong, dominating the first two quarters and taking a 9-0 lead into halftime. My one-yard touchdown run, followed by a field goal from Greg Ashworth, had us feeling confident.

But the second half was a different story. Fumbles and interceptions plagued us, and the Mavericks took full advantage of every mistake we made. They rallied back and ended up defeating us 17-9, handing us our second loss of the season. I led the team in rushing with 71 yards on 17 carries, but it wasn't enough to overcome our turnovers. Rob Miller chipped in 29 yards on 11 carries, but we left Omaha frustrated and eager to redeem ourselves in our next game.

As we approached our eighth game of the year, we traveled to Maryville to face Northwest Missouri State College's JV team. This time, our versatility on the field, especially in the kicking game, helped us secure a 16-13 victory. The game started off promising when I scored on a four-yard run with just under two minutes remaining in the second quarter, giving us a 7-0 lead at halftime. But Northwest came out firing in the second half, tying the game at 7-7 with a spectacular 95-yard touchdown pass

Chapter Six

with 5:59 left in the third quarter.

Despite the big play from Northwest, we didn't back down. Jeff Landen nailed a 40-yard field goal with 2:45 left in the third quarter to give us a 10-7 lead. We continued to grind, and Greg Ashworth followed up with an 18-yard field goal to extend our lead to 13-7. Although Northwest threatened late in the game, it was Ashworth who sealed the win with a final 30-yard field goal with just over eight minutes left in the fourth quarter, giving us a 16-13 victory. It was a close game, but our special teams came through when it mattered most. I had a strong performance, leading the team with 29 carries for 148 yards, and Carl Boldra had a great day in the air, completing 15 of 25 passes for 199 yards.

Coach Marty Allen was proud of our resilience. With that win, we set a new school record for the number of victories in a season. At 7-2, we confidently headed into our next matchup against the North Dakota School of Science. It was another dominating performance, as we shut them down 29-7 in a non-conference game. Once again, our offense was clicking, and Carl Boldra connected with Jan Demby for a 67-yard touchdown strike, followed by a 27-yard touchdown to Greg Dan. Greg Ashworth added both extra points, extending our lead to 14-0. By the third quarter, the score had ballooned to 26-0, with our defense holding strong.

I had another solid game, contributing to the ground attack, but the overall team effort made the difference. With the victory, we improved to 8-2, which was the best record the Scotties had seen since 1956. We had one game left, and it was a chance to break the school record for wins in a season.

The Stakes Kept Rising

In our final game, we hosted the Benedictine JV squad. It was a game that showcased our dominance from start to finish. Dennis McGovern opened the scoring with a 59-yard touchdown run, giving us a 6-0 lead after the first half. Greg Ashworth added another field goal, and then Carl Boldra hit Randy Davis with a 30-yard touchdown pass to extend the lead to 19-0. Our defense and special teams continued to shine, as John Paul Towbley returned a punt 32 yards for a touchdown, and Jan Demby opened the fourth quarter with a 22-yard touchdown run.

By the time McGovern added his final score, we had put the game away, winning 32-0 and finishing the season with an impressive 9-2 record. I finished the game with 63 yards rushing, which pushed my season total over 1,000 yards. It was a great way to end the year, and we had made our mark in the history books.

Looking back, that season was about more than just wins and losses—it was about overcoming adversity, playing as a team, and setting new standards for Highland Community College football. From our early victories to the heartbreaking losses, we proved our resilience and left a legacy that would be remembered for years to come.

In 1984, I had a season to remember at Highland Community College, tallying 1,025 rushing yards on 205 carries, with an impressive 14 touchdowns. These stats weren't just numbers; they symbolized grit, determination, and countless hours of training. My ability to break tackles, weave through defenders, and explode with speed made me a dominant force on the field. That year, I led the entire junior college division in all-purpose yardage, averaging a staggering 178 yards per game.

Chapter Six

As the final whistle blew on my Highland career, I cemented myself in the record books, holding the all-time career record for carries at 324, standing second in career rushing yards with 1,865, and ranking third in points scored with 144. My relentless performance throughout the season earned me All-American honors as an all-purpose back—an achievement that still holds a special place in my heart. The records I set during that season still stand to this day as a testament to the hard work and passion I poured into every game.

The 1984 season wasn't just memorable because of individual accolades, though. For the first time, my brother Jeff and I realized a childhood dream: playing on the same football team. The Barbee brothers shared the backfield, making it a truly special season for our family. Jeff had always been my biggest supporter, but the stakes were different when we lined up together at Highland. I'll never forget the first day of practice when each player had to stand up and introduce themselves. Jeff confidently stood and declared, "I'm here to take my brother's position." It was a bold statement, and it caught everyone's attention.

Jeff gave it his all, but when the coaches pulled him aside, they had some advice: "If you want playing time, you better switch to fullback." After some thought, Jeff made the decision to switch. He became the starting fullback while I remained at tailback. Together, we formed the Barbee backfield—a dream come true for both of us and a proud moment for our family.

Of course, football wasn't the only adventure we had in Highland. One story that sticks out took place at the local bar, "Ernie's," which was the go-to spot in town. Ernie's wasn't just a smoky dive bar but a place where the locals and students mingled. The front of the bar was usually packed with townies, while the back belonged to the students. It was the kind of place where you could run up a tab, and mysteriously, it seemed like someone always took care of our tabs.

After every game, it was tradition to head to Ernie's, especially for the "Brew Crew." A bunch of us football players paid $20 to join this rowdy group, which allowed us to drink for free before, during, and after home basketball games. Coach Flax, one of our more unconventional supporters, would even buy us a beer keg before the games. We'd show up, already buzzing, and sit in a special section behind the opposing team's bench, relentlessly heckling their players and coaches. It was a wild time, but those nights at Ernie's bonded us as teammates in ways nothing else could.

One particular night, I found myself deep in the action at Ernie's, a little too drunk from the beers we had been downing. A guy was shooting pool and had an easy shot left—a five-inch tap to make the eight ball. Feeling bold, I decided to heckle him. "I bet you can't make that shot," I said, tossing $5 down on the table. Not missing a beat, the guy turned to me and sneered, "I bet your mamma $5 I can make this shot."

Before I could respond, Jeff, who had been watching the whole thing from the other side of the table, stepped up. He didn't say a word. In a split second, Jeff knocked the guy clean out and left him crumpled on the floor. Jeff looked down at him and growled, "His mamma is my mamma. Don't ever talk about our mamma that way." The bar fell silent for a moment, and then, just like

Chapter Six

that, the commotion picked back up. Jeff had once again stepped in to protect me, just like he always had.

That night was just one of many that made our time at Highland unforgettable. From breaking records on the field to forming lasting memories with my brother and teammates, 1984 was a year that shaped me not only as a football player but as a person. After Highland, I continued my career at Peru State College in Nebraska, but the lessons I learned and the bonds I formed at Highland will stay with me forever.

Chapter SEVEN

THE FALL: LOSING IT ALL

The Descent into Darkness

The struggle is real, and the word "struggle" doesn't even begin to capture the depths of it. Addiction is a relentless force, its grip as powerful as it is insidious. It takes root deep within the mind, rewiring thoughts and decisions until it becomes nearly impossible to distinguish between yourself and the addiction that has overtaken you. Scientists say addiction literally reshapes the brain's pathways, and I lived that reality firsthand.

It started innocently enough. I was just a boy, no more than eight or nine, when my Uncle Bob took me fishing. That day, he forgot to bring anything for me to drink. His solution? A can of Busch beer. It wasn't much, but it was enough—a knock on the door that opened up a path I wouldn't realize I was walking down until much

Chapter Seven

later. At the time, it felt harmless. I wasn't even thinking about what it might lead to; I was just a kid, happy to be spending time with my uncle. But that one drink planted a seed, one that would sprout years later into something much darker.

Fast forward to my senior year of high school in 1982. By then, the drinking age was 18, and it wasn't hard to get beer. I remember Friday mornings like they happened yesterday. My classmates and I would hit Johnny's Tavern, the doors opening at 7 AM. We'd drink two, maybe three pitchers of beer before heading to school, buzzing as we walked through the halls. We thought we were untouchable, that showing up to class with a light buzz was just another way to show we were living life to the fullest. And in the moment, it felt fun—there's no denying that. But those fun times were laying the foundation for years of struggle. If I could go back, I would trade every single one of those so-called "good times" to avoid the pain that followed.

Friday nights brought keg parties out in the country. We'd get sloppy drunk, stumbling, falling, and laughing through the haze of it all. The mornings after were rough—waking up with no idea what happened the night before, trying to piece together the night through the fog of a hangover. Then came the "freedom" of college football, a new chapter where the party only escalated. Wednesday nights turned into wild midweek bashes, and by Friday and Saturday, it was a full-blown blackout. I was convincing myself that this was the time of my life—that this was what college was all about. But underneath the bravado, I was sinking deeper and deeper into addiction. The scholarship I had worked so hard for? Gone. Lost to alcohol, bad decisions, and a GPA that

The Fall: Losing It All

couldn't keep me afloat.

That should have been my wake-up call. Losing the scholarship should have screamed at me that it was time to get help, time to turn things around. But the addiction was already in full control, and instead of facing reality, I doubled down.

In January of 1985, I transferred to Peru State College in Nebraska, thinking it was a fresh start. But in truth, I just carried my destructive habits with me. By then, it wasn't just alcohol—it was weed, too. I'd smoke before class, after class, and even between classes, numbing myself to the consequences that were piling up around me. I'll never forget one night when I woke up in a dorm room, disoriented, with two men standing over me. They told me I had been drunk and was causing trouble on campus.

The next day, I found myself on behavioral probation. The message was clear: one more slip-up, and I'd be out. But did that stop me? No. I kept partying, living in a haze of denial, ignoring the fact that my life was slowly spiraling out of control.

Around that time, I started seeing a girl, SB. Our relationship was intense and reckless, fueled by our mutual struggles and the wild college atmosphere. It was more than just casual dating; we were deeply involved, physically and emotionally. Things took a drastic turn when, in June, my mother called me out of the blue. SB had called her, crying. She was in California for the summer, and something was obviously wrong. When I got her on the phone, all she could say was, "I'm sorry. I'm so sorry." Over and over again. At first, I didn't understand

Chapter Seven

what she meant. Then, the truth hit me like a freight train—she was pregnant.

I was speechless, blindsided by the reality of what she was saying. SB's parents were furious. Her father was the dean at Peru State, and they flew out to California, forcing her to have an abortion. I'll never forget the night her father called me. His voice was cold and final. "It's done," he said, before hanging up the phone. When I called him back, he made it crystal clear that if I set foot on Peru State's campus again, I'd face more trouble than I could handle. His threat wasn't subtle—it was a promise. That summer of 1985 was one of the hardest of my life.

I was at home, trying to prepare for the upcoming football season, but my mind was a mess. I worked out every day, jogging to the gym, but the weight of everything that had happened sat on my shoulders. My future was uncertain, and I had a child that would never be born, a reality that haunted me.

The struggle wasn't just about alcohol or drugs—it was about the loss, the regret, and the realization that addiction had robbed me of so much. And yet, I wasn't ready to admit defeat. The battle was far from over.

After working a grueling 12-hour shift at Kmart's distribution center in Lawrence, Kansas, I found myself unwinding at Johnny's Tavern with my buddy, Charlie. That morning, we cashed our checks, kicked back a few drinks, and by early afternoon, we were riding on Charlie's motorcycle, the thrill mixing with the alcohol in our veins. It was then that Charlie dropped a sobering thought: "If we keep riding like this, we're going to die."

The Fall: Losing It All

And he wasn't wrong—our state of mind and the bike weren't a good mix.

Thinking we were being responsible, we headed over to Dale Wiley's Ford to rent a car instead of continuing on the motorcycle. As we checked out the options, a customized van caught our eye. "How much for this one?" we asked the salesman. When he said it would be just two dollars more than what we had originally planned, we pooled our money, signed the papers, and got the keys.

The rest of that day, we loaded the van with drugs and beer and hit the streets of Lawrence, hopping from bar to bar, keeping the party alive. But things quickly spiraled, as they often do when you ignore that voice in your head telling you to stop. Eventually, I dropped Charlie off, intending to pick him up later. But instead of heading home, I made the reckless decision to drive to Topeka, all while drinking and getting high.

The road between Topeka and Lawrence blurred as I smoked weed and snorted cocaine, fully lost in the haze of intoxication. By the time I made it back to Lawrence, I hit another bar. By now, I was deep into a blackout, and at some point, I made another bad decision—to drive home. The next thing I remember, I woke up amidst twisted metal and shattered glass. I had slammed the rented van into a telephone pole, totaling it while going about 100 miles per hour.

The steering wheel had me pinned, and battery acid dripped onto my skin. In a daze, I kept repeating to the rescue team, "Just get me out of here. I need out." They worked quickly to free me from the wreckage, and I

Chapter Seven

spent a day or two in the hospital. My mother, despite being out of town, had felt it in her gut that something was wrong. When she called home and heard I had been in an accident, she and my father rushed back to Lawrence.

After picking me up from the hospital, my dad drove me out to the scene of the crash. "Son, I'm going to show you how blessed you truly are," he said. When we arrived, the sight of the wreckage sobered me instantly. Looking at the damage, I realized I shouldn't have survived. There was no explanation other than divine intervention. I knew in that moment that I had been spared for a reason, and it forced me to confront the truth—I had been reckless, disrespecting my own body and life, which was God's temple.

This, along with the other setbacks I had been facing, including an abortion and my accident, made me decide not to return to Peru State in the fall. But just three weeks later, my teammate J.M. from Arkansas broke down five miles outside of Lawrence. My dad woke me up and told me to go pick him up and get his car towed. Once I got J.M., he politely asked if my dad might take him back to Peru State. My father, always willing to help, agreed. Then he turned to me and said, "You're riding along, too."

I didn't want to go. I was still recovering, with my arm bandaged and stitches in my head from the accident. But when my dad used that tone, I knew it wasn't up for debate. So, that Sunday afternoon after church, we drove up to Peru State.

In the fall of 1985, I found myself back at Peru

The Fall: Losing It All

State, though it wasn't how I had imagined. I had already told Coach Adcox that I wasn't going to play football that year, thinking that my focus had shifted. But Coach Adcox didn't give up on me. As we walked together across the practice field one day, he turned to me and said, "Barbee, if you're here next Saturday, I'll give you your full-ride scholarship back." His faith in me sparked something deep inside. That following Sunday, I was back on campus, officially a student again, and back in pads, ready to play the game that had been such a big part of my life.

By the time I rejoined the team, they had already been practicing and were preparing for the next game. Coach Adcox, knowing I hadn't gone through the full conditioning regimen, didn't put me in the starting lineup right away. He did, however, give me a spot on the opening kickoff against Evangel College from Springfield. I spent the entire first quarter on the sidelines, but in the second quarter, I heard Coach's voice, "Barbee, get in the game." My heart raced as I stepped onto the field. The ball was snapped, and on my first carry, I broke free for a 64-yard run. It felt like I was back in my element, like I had never left.

That initial burst of excitement was short-lived, though. After that big play, I didn't see much action for the rest of the game. The next week, we played Tarkio, and I didn't start then either. But my playing time started to increase. During that second game, I finally crossed the goal line, scoring my first touchdown of the season. It felt like I was getting back into the rhythm. By the third game of the season, Coach told me I was ready to start. The excitement I felt leading up to that game against Concordia College was unmatched. I stepped onto the

Chapter Seven

field, determined to have my breakout moment. By the end of the first quarter, I had already gained 72 yards, and I could feel that this was going to be one of those special games.

But just as quickly as that excitement had built, tragedy struck. On the first play of the second quarter, I made a sharp cut, aiming to burst through the hole in the line. I got hit, and instantly, I felt something go wrong in my ankle. All my ligaments were torn, and just like that, I was out of commission for the next three games. When I finally returned, I wasn't anywhere close to 100%. My season fizzled out. I tried to contribute where I could, but it was clear that I wasn't the player I had once been. I was struggling both on and off the field.

Even though I was back in Peru, playing the game I loved, I was still fighting a much deeper battle—my addiction. I had graduated from just drinking and smoking weed to snorting cocaine. It had a grip on me, and I couldn't shake it. The highs, the rush, the euphoria that cocaine gave me—I craved it. And then there were the steroids. I wanted to perform better, to push my body past its limits, but instead, I was sinking deeper into addiction.

The roller coaster came to a devastating halt one morning in May 1986. I woke up to campus police standing over me, telling me I needed to report to the dean's office. I didn't remember a thing from the night before, but apparently, I had gotten blackout drunk and been involved in several fights. It wasn't my first incident, either. I had already been on probation for a previous altercation. Now, with only two weeks left in the semester, I was summoned before the dean. They gave me 48 hours to pack my things and leave campus. In a single night of drunken recklessness, I had thrown it all away—my education, my football career, and my full-ride scholarship.

When I got home, my father called me upstairs. He didn't yell, didn't get angry. He simply asked, "What happened?" I explained everything: the drinking, the blackout, the fights. And all he said was, "It's time for you to go back to work." It was a simple statement, but it carried a weight that hit me harder than any tackle on the field.

My life began spiraling further out of control after that. In August 1986, I got my first DUI and spent my first night in jail. It was a wake-up call, but I ignored it. In May and June of 1987, I received two more DUIs. My addiction was driving my life into the ground, but I was still in denial, convincing myself that I had it all under control. But the truth was, I didn't. The drugs and alcohol had a hold on me, and I was powerless to stop it. As I lost myself to the addiction, the dreams I once had slipped further and further away.

After leaving Peru State, I returned to Lawrence, Kansas, where I spent a couple of years trying to find my footing. In 1988, I served as an assistant football coach at Haskell Indian Junior College (now Haskell Indian Nations University). We had a decent season, finishing with a 6-4 record. It felt good to be involved in football again, but I knew I wasn't where I wanted to be.

Later that year, I made a big decision—I moved to Chicago. I had followed my heart, chasing a romantic relationship that eventually fizzled out. But even though the relationship didn't work out, I stayed in the city. I

Chapter Seven

took on a series of different jobs, doing whatever I could to make ends meet, but slowly, I began to drift into serious trouble with drug addiction. What started as a way to cope with the pressures of life spiraled into a state of mind that eventually led me down the dark road of homelessness.

By the early '90s, I had hit rock bottom. I found myself staying at the Pacific Garden Mission, a Christian-based shelter in the heart of Chicago. I stayed there for six months, attending chapel services, trying to make sense of my life. One day, while handing out religious tracts on the streets, I met a woman named Marie. That meeting changed everything. We connected, and after ten months of dating, we got married in June 1992. Marie was a Chicago public school teacher, and together, we started building a life. We had two beautiful children—Stephen Anthony and Sherell Lynn. Life began to stabilize for me. I had a family, a home, and for the first time in a long time, I felt like things were moving in the right direction.

In 1994, I took on a new challenge and accepted a position as a chaplain at Lawndale Christian Health Center, a Christian-based clinic in the inner city. I worked there for three and a half years, counseling patients and staff, using my life experiences to help others. Around the same time, I enrolled at the Moody Bible Institute in Chicago, where I took classes in biblical studies and theology. I was passionate about deepening my faith and learning more about the Word of God. By 1997, I became the first African-American to serve as the Men's Director at Pacific Garden Mission—the very same shelter where I had once lived. It felt like a full-circle moment, standing in a place that had once been my ref-

The Fall: Losing It All

uge, now offering help and guidance to others in need. I held that position for two years, but eventually, I transitioned to a new role with Featherfist Inc., an organization assisting the homeless in Chicago. I worked there for a year and a half, all while continuing my studies at Trinity International University in Deerfield, Illinois, where I earned a bachelor's degree in communications in 1999.

However, life has a way of throwing hard consequences at you when you least expect them. My oldest brother, Jeff, whom I always saw as an adventurous protector, ended up in prison, serving a 99-year sentence for armed robbery. His fall weighed heavily on me, and in July 2000, my own life took a sharp turn. I separated from my wife, and she moved to St. Louis, taking our two children with her. The pain of that separation pushed me back into my old habits, and I suffered a devastating relapse with drugs and alcohol. Once again, I found myself homeless, bouncing between shelters in Des Moines, Iowa, and Hammond, Indiana. My life had spiraled out of control, and I felt lost.

In July 2001, I returned to Lawrence for what I thought would be a short visit. But the visit turned into years of drifting from job to job and relationship to relationship, all while still struggling with addiction. In the beginning, it felt like just another day, but I knew something was off. The paranoia had been building for years—over half a decade, really. It's not like I hadn't felt the tension in the air, the eyes watching. The streets talk, but I guess I didn't listen closely enough. I was caught up in the game, moving weight, not realizing just how deep things were getting for me.

Chapter Seven

Chapter EIGHT

THE COLLAPSE: FROM HERO TO INMATE

By 2005, Lawrence, Kansas, had turned into a maze of distribution spots. I wasn't the mastermind, just a cog in the machine, but that didn't matter in the grand scheme. The DEA had their eyes on all of us. I had known Lester for a while. At the time, I didn't see the signs—the way he shifted, how he looked at me like I was already a ghost. It was just a ride to 2408 Alabama, another drop, another day. He didn't flinch when he gave me a ride there. Now I know why.

July 22, 2005. I remember that day clearly. Lester had set it all up and made it seem like business as usual. I took the $100 and walked into the apartment, A-10. It was almost routine. One gram of crack cocaine, easy enough. What I didn't know—what I couldn't know—was that this whole thing was a setup. The money exchanged hands, and I brought the product back, handed

Chapter Eight

it off. The undercover officer played it cool, and I played the fool.

$20. That's what I got out of it. Twenty dollars to run the risk of my life crashing down. I left that exchange thinking nothing of it, but it wasn't long before the walls started closing in. Five days later, on July 27, they stormed the place. The raid came hard and fast at 2408 Alabama. I wasn't there when the door came crashing down, but I could feel it. It was like the world knew what was happening before I even got word.

The evidence was everywhere—plastic bags, digital scales, cash stashed in every corner. 3.43 grams of coke, 88.62 grams of crack. The weight of it all was suffocating. But the kicker? The fingerprints. They found fingerprints on the packaging. That packaging was my link to all of it, like leaving my signature on my own demise. It's funny how something as small as a fingerprint can be the link to convict and put people away for many years.

Everything after that was a blur—court dates, hearings, the slow realization that I was now a number, a name on a case file. *The United States versus Stephen Barbee.* It's a strange thing to see your name stacked up against the government like that, to know they've been watching you for years, piecing together your life in bits and pieces, waiting for the perfect moment to strike.

Looking back, I realize how much was at play, how I was part of something bigger than I understood. The streets have a way of pulling you in, making you think you're invincible. But in the end, it all comes crashing down. The weight of those years—2000 to 2006—pressed down on me like a judge's gavel. Every decision,

The Collapse: From Hero to Inmate

every handoff, every dollar earned or lost, led to this moment.

Now, as I sit here reflecting, I can't help but think of how easily things could have gone differently. That CI, that ride to Alabama Street, the fingerprints—it all feels like a series of small steps that led me to the edge. And when I stepped over, there was no going back.

By the summer of 2005, I was using drugs on a daily basis, completely unaware that one of the locations where I bought drugs was under federal investigation. Twice in July, I was seen at this location, but I was too far gone to realize the danger I was in. It was a cold December morning when everything shifted.

December 18, 2007—I'll never forget the way that date felt like a door slamming shut. For years, I had felt the pressure building, but I always thought I could stay a step ahead. I had no idea that while I was trying to maneuver through the streets, the Feds were right there, putting the pieces together, quietly watching, and waiting. And then came the sealed indictment.

The apartment—it wasn't just a random spot. It was a hub, a place where people came and went, a place filled with ghosts of the choices I had made. I knew the game. I knew the risk, but what I didn't expect was how deeply the net had already been cast. There were personal items left behind by people, remnants of lives we barely paid attention to. We were all part of the same tangled web, a collection of known drug users, hustlers, and middlemen, coming and going like clockwork. None of us thought about how close we were being watched, how the walls had ears.

Chapter Eight

When the surveillance started, I couldn't tell you. Was it months? Years? The paranoia that sinks into your bones when you know something's off but can't quite place it, that's what eats at you. It wasn't just my life they were tracking—it was everyone who came through that door, everyone who had a piece of the puzzle in their pocket. The apartment was like a stage, and we were the cast, performing without knowing the curtains had already been pulled back.

When the search warrant came down, it was almost a relief in a twisted way. It was like the waiting was finally over, like the tension that had been gnawing at me for years had finally stopped. I knew my days felt numbered, but I did not know everyone around me would sink at the same time with me. They had us pegged, all of us.

When I got hit with counts one, four, and fifteen, it was like my heart stopped. December 18, 2007, that's the day the world came crashing down. It's strange how this piece of paper signified a turning point in my freedom. It was a clinical read, a matter-of-fact tone, with no love; to read the charges aloud felt heavy.

It was like being caught in a storm you didn't see coming, knowing that no matter how hard you tried, there was no escaping the consequences.

I can't describe the feeling of knowing that your fate has been decided without you even being in the room. It felt haunted down like an animal, caged in by choices I couldn't take back or undo.

That's the thing they don't tell you when you're

deep in the game—the moment you lose control, it's not loud. It's silent. It's a sealed indictment sitting on a desk somewhere, waiting for the right moment to turn your world upside down.

THE LEGAL BATTLE BEGINS

December 18, 2007—that date is burned into my memory like a scar. It was the day everything collapsed, the day I was arrested and slapped with a charge that felt like a death sentence. Five kilos of crack cocaine. Ten years to life. I remember sitting there, numb, barely able to process the weight of it all. Ten years… Life. The numbers echoed in my head like a drumbeat, over and over, until I couldn't hear anything else.

I should've been in full-blown panic mode, but the truth is, I felt detached, like I was watching someone else's life fall apart. It was like looking at myself from outside my body, seeing the walls close in but unable to move or to fight. Despair doesn't hit all at once—it creeps up, seeping into your bones until you can't shake it. And by the time I was released on bond that same day, I could feel it settling in, thick and heavy like a fog.

Chapter Nine

The conditions of my bond, the constant supervision by pretrial services, felt like a leash, a constant reminder that I wasn't free, not really. Every court date, every hearing felt like a punch to the gut, a fresh wave of hopelessness. I thought Jackie R., my lawyer at the time, would fight for me, but even that started to feel like a lost cause. Every time we went to court, it was like being stuck in a nightmare I couldn't wake up from. The motions, the back-and-forth, the endless waiting. February 4, another hearing, and once again, the charges were rearranged, refiled—back to five kilos, back to the same crushing reality. Ten years to life.

I couldn't breathe. I was drowning in the possibility of never walking free again. When they assigned me a new lawyer, Jackie R, nothing within me changed. The experience felt the same, although the face I saw failing me remained. It wasn't good or bad lawyering, it was just my fate. It didn't matter who stood beside me in court—nothing felt real anymore. My life had been reduced to courtrooms and legal jargon, my future tied up in paperwork and motions I barely understood. Depression doesn't always announce itself with loud sobs or breakdowns. Sometimes, it's the quiet, the endless monotony of feeling trapped in a cage you built yourself. That's where I was.

And then came February 9, 2008. My lawyer, Jackie R., the one I thought I could maybe rely on, was forced to step down due to a conflict of interest. Another blow. It was like the ground beneath me kept shifting, making it impossible to find solid footing. Now, a new judge and a new lawyer—another fresh start that felt like the beginning of the end.

The Legal Battle Begins

March 31, 2008—another court hearing, another motion status, another date scribbled into my memory. They just continued the case again. I was stuck in this legal limbo, waiting for a hammer to drop, not knowing when or how hard it would hit. Every time I walked out of that courtroom, I felt smaller, more broken. It's hard to describe the kind of weight that presses down on your soul when you're facing the possibility of losing everything—your freedom, your future, your hope.

I remember sitting in that courtroom, staring at the ceiling, feeling nothing but emptiness. Deep despair doesn't look like crying or screaming. It's silent. It's the feeling of being hollowed out, of knowing that no matter how many new lawyers or judges they assign, no one could fix the mess I was in.

I was lost in it all. Each passing day, each new hearing felt like another nail in the coffin. Depression weighed on me like an anchor, dragging me deeper into myself. I couldn't see a way out, I couldn't imagine a life beyond this cycle of hearings and motions. The hope I once had was gone, replaced with a cold acceptance that maybe this was it. Maybe I wasn't going to make it out of this after all.

The judge's voice rang out as they pulled my bond. I tested positive for cocaine at the mission where I was supposed to be finding refuge and redemption. April 13, 2008—that date felt seared into my memory like a scar. It was just one more mark on the timeline of my failure.

I had been released on bond, under the watchful eye of pretrial services, on May 12, 2008. I had been given another chance, but my actions, my inability to stay

Chapter Nine

clean, shattered any hope I had. They said I had admitted to using $40 worth of crack cocaine on April 26, 2008, and I couldn't deny it. The truth was like a noose tightening around my neck. I had tried to defend myself, submitted to the urine tests, only for it to come back positive, confirming what I already knew deep down.

I used on April 25, 2008—crack cocaine again. The habit that had me by the throat wouldn't let go, even after inpatient rehab, even after facing the stark reality that I was losing everything. I admitted it to my supervising probation officer. It wasn't the first time, and it wouldn't be the last. March 13, 2008—I'd used crack twice after being released from rehab. The guilt, the shame, it was like a cycle I couldn't break, no matter how hard I tried to outrun it.

And the alcohol… God, the alcohol.

I remember downing that pint of vodka on April 19, 2008. It numbed the pain, but only for a moment. April 28, May 3, May 8—dates when the vodka flowed freely again, drowning out the little bit of hope I still had left. I couldn't stop, even when I knew it would cost me everything. I missed the urine tests on May 6 and May 8. I didn't show up for counseling at Vallejo on June 3. I had become my own worst enemy, spiraling deeper into the darkness that had swallowed my life.

When they revoked my bond, I wasn't surprised. I stood there, hollow inside, knowing I had failed. The investigation report from the Douglas County Drug Enforcement Unit and the U.S. Attorney painted a picture of a man who had lost control, a man whose promises to get clean were as hollow as the echoing footsteps in that

The Legal Battle Begins

cold courtroom. And that man was me.

This was my deep disgrace as they transported me to the Community Correction of America in Leavenworth, Kansas, a federal detention center. My life was once again at a crossroads, and I knew the road ahead wouldn't be easy.

Sitting in my prison cell, I began to ask myself the toughest question: *Where am I, and how did I get here?* It was a moment of brutal honesty, an unmasking of all the lies I had told myself over the years. I had lived a life of compartmentalization, wearing different masks based on my surroundings—the addict, the athlete, the family man, the man of faith—each one covering the truth of who I was and what I had become. But the time had come to confront reality, to tear down those walls I had built up.

I knew that the first step in walking in my calling was swearing off drugs and alcohol for good. As I sat there in my cell, I asked myself a simple, but life-changing question: *How many times was I arrested sober?* The answer was clear: never. Every time I found myself in handcuffs, drugs and alcohol were involved. I made a decision right then and there—if I could just stay off the substances, I would never have to wear those silver handcuffs again. But I knew it wouldn't stop there. The journey I was embarking on would require more than just sobriety—it would demand a complete transformation, from the inside out.

In prison, my work assignment was to help with

religious services. Ironically, what started as a simple job turned into the foundation of my spiritual rebirth. I learned about many different faiths, which only served to strengthen my own. I found myself praying with inmates and even prison lieutenants. There was a palpable sense of God's provision at every turn, from finances to favor with the guards. But what really struck me was the inner transformation I began to experience.

One day, the Holy Spirit confronted me in a way I couldn't ignore. I realized how, for most of my life, I had believed the enemy's lie: *When you're in church, God loves you, but when you're in the crack house, He doesn't.* It was a twisted mindset that kept me shackled to guilt and shame. But in that moment, I heard God's voice clearly: *I'm still the God that loves you when you're in your feelings. I'm still the God who loves you when you're in church. I'm still the God who loves you when you have a career. And I still love you when you're out there in the drug world.*

We can build these walls, but also choose to let them fall down. You have to tear them down because God didn't put them there. He loves and forgives you. It was a revelation that changed everything. I wasn't just being called to stop using drugs—I was being called to walk in the fullness of God's love for me, no matter where I had been.

The federal judicial system is different from the state system in many ways, and I was learning that firsthand. I was held at the Community Corrections of America (CCA) facility in Leavenworth, Kansas, a federal detention center housing close to 1,500 inmates. It was a place of waiting—waiting for court dates, waiting for sentencing, waiting for freedom.

Chapter TEN

THE FEDERAL PRISON SENTENCE

On August 28, 2009, I was sentenced to a 70-month prison term for one controlled sale of $100 worth of crack cocaine to a confidential informant. That's right—just $100 landed me nearly six years in prison. It seemed surreal, but this was my reality now.

While the days in my cell were often filled with quiet reflection, the hardest times were the moments of isolation, not hearing from family or friends. It's a painful truth the way people distance themselves when you're incarcerated. Those you thought were close often fade away. But to my surprise, one person consistently reached out—Mother Holloman, a woman I hadn't expected to hear from. Her letters were like lifelines to me, words of encouragement that filled my soul when I felt abandoned.

Chapter Ten

I still remember her letters vividly. One, dated October 16, 2009, started with, *Dear Reverend Barbee, I hope you're settling into your new place by now.* She told me about life back home, the church events, and the pastor appreciation programs. Her words were simple, yet they carried profound meaning for me. *We pray God will continue to use you right where you are planted for now.* Those words, "planted for now," struck me deeply. It made me realize that even though I was behind bars, God had a purpose for me there.

Her next letter, dated October 24, 2009, was equally uplifting. She told me about the church's upcoming events and how they had been praying for me to be released under the new laws. But more than that, she reminded me of the power I had to influence the young men around me, encouraging me to tutor them and point them to Christ. Her letters came with old sermon outlines from Pastor Holloman, little pieces of wisdom that I clung to as if they were gold.

Mother Holloman's letters, coupled with my journaling, helped me stay grounded. She reminded me that even though I was physically locked up, I didn't have to be spiritually or emotionally imprisoned. Her unwavering faith and encouragement kept me going, and I held onto her words during some of my darkest days.

Looking back, it was in those moments of isolation and reflection that the real unmasking happened. I had spent so many years hiding from myself and from God. But in that prison cell, with nowhere to run and nothing left to lose, I found a freedom I had never known. The walls I had built to compartmentalize my life came crumbling down, and I finally began to walk in the truth of

The Federal Prison Sentence

who I was—flawed, yes, but loved by God nonetheless.

As I sit here and reflect on my journey, it's hard not to ask the question: *Where am I, and how did I get here?* Today, I'm at FCI Pekin, a federal prison in Illinois. I've been here since September 2009, but my real journey—one of enlightenment, humility, and soul-searching—began long before that. It was on August 28, 2009, when I was sentenced to 70 months in prison, but in truth, I had been locked up since May 2008, both physically and spiritually. Back then, I was consumed with self-centeredness, my mind playing the "blame game." I pointed fingers at everyone but myself, refusing to accept responsibility for my actions. But slowly, God began to peel back the layers of my hardened heart, revealing hard truths about myself that I could no longer deny.

Each day, I'm learning to let go of the things that once bound me—pride, anger, addiction, and the need for control. I am now understanding that part of my journey here is about learning to trust God completely, to let go of my will, and surrender to Him. He's delivering me, not just from the confines of these prison walls, but from myself.

Mother Holloman's letters have been my constant companions, offering encouragement, love, and reminders that God still has a plan for my life. On December 12, 2009, she wrote to me, *"Merry Christmas Reverend Barbee, I was so happy to receive your letter and rejoice to hear how the Lord is using you."* Her words, filled with faith and hope, pierced through the gloom of my incarceration. She reminded me that, despite my circumstances, God's plans for me were still great. She said, *"Keep the faith, stay true to Him, and He will use you*

Chapter Ten

more than He ever has before." Those words lifted my spirit and gave me a renewed sense of purpose. It was as if God was using her to remind me that my story wasn't over, that my current situation was just a chapter, not the whole book.

Even through the cold Kansas winters, as Mother Holloman shared about snowstorms that canceled church services, she would always find a way to offer warmth through her letters. In January 2010, she wrote, *"Praise the Lord, it's finally above freezing here. The sun is shining, and I am so grateful for that."* Her gratitude in the midst of harsh weather reminded me of the importance of finding light even in dark places. That's what her letters were—light. She would speak of church activities, Pastor Holloman's sermons, and how she was praying daily for my release, praying that the new laws would bring me back to them sooner than expected.

On April 29, 2010, I found myself once again asking, *Where am I?* But this time, the question wasn't born out of confusion or frustration. It was a deeper, more spiritual question. God had been working on me. I could feel it. I wrote, *"God is so good. I am learning more and more to trust the Lord."* People had disappointed me, yes, but through it all, I was discovering that God was always there, shaping me, guiding me, and preparing me for the next chapter of my life.

I had been surrounded by negativity, by strongholds of unforgiveness, division, and bitterness. Yet, through it all, God was calling me to rise above, to die to myself, to let go of my own desires, and to submit to His will. I could feel His presence, even in the cold, steel confines of the prison. He was teaching me lessons that couldn't

The Federal Prison Sentence

be learned anywhere else, lessons about patience, forgiveness, and true transformation.

"Lord, what lessons have you taught me here?" I found myself asking over and over. Each day in that cell, I saw more clearly that this was about so much more than just serving time. It was about preparing me for something greater. God was using this season to prune away the parts of me that no longer served His purpose—my pride, my addictions, my need for control. I began to understand that freedom wasn't just about walking out of prison one day; it was about walking in the freedom that only God can give, no matter where I was.

The letters from Mother Holloman, the journal entries, the quiet prayers—all of it was preparing me for the next step. It was as if God was whispering to me, *"This isn't the end. There is still work to be done, and I am not finished with you yet."*

So here I sit, in a place where the world might see only bars and walls. But in my heart, I know I am being shaped by the hands of the Creator. He is preparing me for a new chapter, one that will be written with hope, with faith, and with the promise that I am more than my past mistakes. God is redeeming every broken piece of my story, using it for His glory.

As I await what comes next, I stand firm in the knowledge that God's plans for me are still unfolding. Each day is a step toward becoming the man He created me to be—a man fully transformed, fully surrendered, and fully alive in Christ.

Chapter Ten

May 11, 2010

As I sit here reading Mother Holloman's letter, I'm reminded of the strength of community—the way people of faith come together to lift one another up, even in the most trying times. Her words are like a balm to my soul, speaking life and encouragement into a place where hope can sometimes feel far away. She opens with an apology for her delay in writing, but I can feel the warmth of her spirit shining through as she shares updates about life at the New Beginning Church. Even in retirement, she says, responsibilities pile up, and she wonders if maybe she's just moving slower.

I can almost hear her laughing at herself as she writes that. Enclosed with her letter is the monthly newsletter. As I hold the paper in my hands, I imagine the life that's unfolding back at the church—the children's ministry, the new men's group, the music and prayer ministries springing up like new blossoms in a garden. These ministries are more than just programs; they are lifelines, bringing people closer to God, offering purpose and direction, and providing spaces where the lost can be found.

The day before Mother's Day, the drama team put on a play called *Mama's Little Jewels,* written by Sister Williams. Mother Holloman writes about the turnout, about how the men of the church served dinner and turned what could have been an ordinary gathering into a night of blessing. I can see the laughter, the joy, the smiles shared across the room as families came together to honor the mothers in their lives. It's a picture of God's grace—how, even in the midst of life's challenges, there are still moments of celebration, still moments where

The Federal Prison Sentence

love shines through.

But then she shares something that makes me sit up a little straighter, something that gives me a fresh perspective on the power of faith. Pastor and Mother Washington are busy working on a pro-life CD, set to debut in June. The songs, written by Mother Washington, aim to open the eyes of the black churches about the devastating effects of abortion on our community. As I read this, I'm struck by the boldness of their mission, the way they're using their gifts to shine light into dark places. It reminds me that God has a purpose for all of us, even when we're facing the toughest of circumstances.

Mother Holloman's words about keeping my eyes fixed on the Lord hit home. *"We are well aware that the Lord is using you in this difficult time for His glory,"* she writes. *"Keep looking to Him when the days are long and hard. He will send you His comfort."* And in this moment, I feel that comfort. It's as if her letter, though filled with news of life outside these walls, carries with it a piece of the Holy Spirit, reminding me that I am not forgotten, that God's plans for me are still in motion.

The letter closes with a beautiful surprise. Reverend Miles proposed to Desiree Washington at the end of service on Mother's Day. As Mother Holloman describes how he got down on one knee, I can see it all unfolding in my mind—the congregation gasping in surprise, Desiree's eyes widening with joy, and Reverend Miles' voice trembling with excitement as he asks her to marry him. The proposal was unexpected, a moment filled with love and hope, a reminder that God's timing is always perfect.

Chapter Ten

The image of Pastor guiding them, counseling them to do things "God's way," is powerful. It's a testament to the importance of wise counsel. Of how waiting on the Lord, and of trusting that His plans for our lives are greater than we could ever imagine.

Mother Holloman's letter is more than just words on a page—it's a reminder that life is still moving, that God is still working, and that even though I am here, in this place, I am still part of something much bigger. The ministries back at the church, the love stories unfolding, the songs being written—they are all a reflection of God's hand at work in the world. And even here, in the stillness of this prison, I know that His hand is at work in my life too.

As I fold the letter and tuck it away with the others, I breathe in deeply, feeling a renewed sense of purpose. This season, as hard as it has been, is not the end of my story. God is still writing it. And like Pastor Washington's pro-life songs, like Reverend Miles' proposal, like the new ministries blossoming at New Beginning Church, my story is one of redemption, of hope, of transformation.

Mother Holloman's words stay with me, echoing in my mind: *"Keep looking to Him when the days are long and hard. He will send you His comfort."* Today, I feel that comfort. And with it, I find the strength to keep moving forward, one day at a time, trusting that God is with me, that He has a plan, and that He will see me through to the other side.

June 6, 2010

As I sit here today, in the chapel at Pekin, Illinois, I feel an overwhelming sense of gratitude. The walls of this place, usually so cold and rigid, seem to melt away in the warmth of God's presence. His hand has been at work in my life in ways I could never have imagined, and today, I'm filled with joy, peace, and excitement. The Lord has been so faithful in His continued restoration of my spirit, even in this season of confinement.

It was three weeks ago, on May 18, 2010, during one of my quiet times with the Lord. His voice was clear as He instructed me to write down the development of something He was preparing in me—prayer. He was guiding me to craft a prayer chain for each of the days here at Pekin. As I reflected on this, I knew it was for His glory and a way for me to stay connected to Him by covering this place in prayer. As the chain grew, I could sense His purpose being fulfilled. Prayer became more than a daily ritual; it became a lifeline, anchoring me in His promises.

June 7, 2010

During our 12:30 service yesterday, the atmosphere in the chapel was electric with God's presence. It was as though His spirit had descended upon us in a powerful, tangible way. As I stood among my fellow inmates, 13 men rose from their seats, giving their lives to the Lord. I could hardly contain my joy as they expressed their desire to be baptized. The room, usually filled with heaviness and despair, was alive with hope and transformation. It felt like the heavens themselves had opened, and the grace of God was pouring down upon us.

Chapter Ten

It was a moment I will never forget—a reminder that even here, in the depths of this prison, God's light shines bright. These men, who had been lost, were now found. They had come to the end of themselves and found Jesus waiting for them with open arms. The excitement of witnessing lives changed in such a profound way filled my heart with renewed purpose. God was moving, and I knew He wasn't done yet.

But life, as it often does, brings its challenges even in the midst of spiritual victories. Two weeks ago, I received an email from Seretha. She has moved on with her life, and while the news stung at first, God spoke to me at that moment. He reminded me of Isaiah 43:18-19, that He was doing a new thing in my life. I cannot go back to the old, to anything from my former life before getting locked up. Just as Paul said, I must forget those things which are behind. God is calling me to move forward, to embrace the new life He is creating for me. It was a bittersweet realization, but it was also freeing. I trust that God's plans for me are far greater than anything I could hold onto from the past.

June 13, 2010

A letter arrived from Pastor and Mother Holloman today, accompanied by the New Beginning Church newsletter. Their words brought both joy and sorrow. They shared the sad news that Pastor Holloman has been diagnosed with Alzheimer's. My heart ached as I read that he's no longer able to get around as he used to. But their faith is unwavering. They are leaning on the Lord, trusting Him more than they trust the medical profession. *"We know who is really in charge,"* Mother Holloman wrote. Her strength is inspiring, a reminder that even in the face of such challenges, we must keep our eyes fixed on God.

On a brighter note, their family celebrated the birth of a granddaughter on Pastor Holloman's 85th birthday, May 25. What a gift that must have been, a reminder of the cycle of life—how even in seasons of loss and illness, God gives us moments of new beginnings. As I read about their lush, green garden, the flowers blooming in every color, I could almost smell the rain-drenched earth and see the vibrant hues. It's amazing how even the simplest things, like the beauty of nature, can remind us of God's faithfulness and provision.

Pastor and Mother Washington also released their pro-life CD, *A Cry for the Unborn,* on May 26. This project, aimed at the black community, is shedding light on the tragic impact of abortion, which has become the number one killer of the black race. As Mother Holloman mentioned, my father has long been a warrior for the unborn, and I pray that this ministry takes off in ways that bring lasting change and awareness. The urgency of their mission resonates deeply with me, as I reflect on how God can use any platform to speak truth and save lives.

In closing, they asked me to pray for the ministry and shared how they tried to reach me by email but encountered some issues. I'll need to follow up and make sure everything is in order. They also mentioned the troubles at KU and the potential for changes in the Big 12, possibly even losing Coach Self. As much as I enjoy following sports, especially my Jayhawks, my heart is more focused on what God is doing in my life and in the lives of those around me.

Chapter Ten

As I reflect on this season, I can't help but feel a deep sense of peace. Despite the hardships, the separations, and the unknowns, God is here. He is present in every moment, guiding me, teaching me, and preparing me for what lies ahead. I am excited for the future, trusting that when I step out from behind these walls, I will not return to the old but will walk fully into the new life He has prepared for me.

June 16, 2010

Another day unfolds here at Pekin, and as I sit in this cell, I am reminded of how much I need to keep being broken before God. The walls around me are a constant reminder of where *me* has gotten me. My worst enemy, the man I once was, is what led me here. But I know God is working, even in this place. Each day is a battle, not just against the bars and the confinement, but against the old self—the self that got me here. I can't go back. I don't want to be that man anymore. The only thing constant in my life is Christ. Family and circumstances change, but He remains the same.

I'm ready to leave Pekin, but as of now, there's still no word on my designation. Patience is tough here, but I know God is calling me to wait, to trust, and to lean into His timing. It's hard not to judge the men around me for their actions, but God is teaching me compassion. I see the anger, hatred, and deceit in the eyes of men here. The violence and foul language are everywhere, but I'm reminded that prison doesn't change a man—only God can. Without Him, there's no hope for real transformation.

So I pray. I pray without ceasing, without knowing

what lies ahead. I pray because it's the only thing I have. I pray because I know the Spirit is at work, even when I can't see it. Every day, I ask God to help me decrease so that He can increase in my life.

June 18, 2010

Yesterday, God showed His faithfulness again. During my drug treatment class, one of the staff members made a comment that stuck with me. She said, *"Mr. Barbee, your integrity speaks for who you are today."* Those words hit me hard. They reminded me of how far God has brought me and how He is continuing to take me from glory to glory. There's no more room for gray areas in my life. I don't want to live in the shadows of compromise any longer. I want to be Christ-like in every situation, in everything I do. That's my prayer.

I'm beginning to understand more deeply that *"there"* is a place of seeking, a place where I meet God not on my terms, but His. I can't keep looking for Him in the old, familiar places—those same places of sin and compromise. I used to want God to walk in my ways, but now I know it's me who has to walk in His. It's not about what I know but who I know, and who is Jesus Christ.

God is calling me into deeper waters, into places I've never been. And I have to be willing to follow Him there, no matter how uncomfortable it makes me. I can feel the unbelief that sometimes creeps in, holding me back from fully trusting Him. But I know I can't limit God. I'm ready to step out into the deep and trust that wherever He leads, His glory is there waiting for me.

Chapter Ten

July 12, 2010

Dear Reverend Barbee,

I apologize that your birthday card didn't reach you on time, but I hope you had a blessed day nonetheless. We pray that God continues to use you mightily where you are. It was wonderful to hear from you, and we've been using your prayer schedule faithfully. What a blessing it has been to pray over those needs every day. Nothing much has changed here, but your newsletters continue to encourage us. If you no longer wish to receive them, just let us know.

We do have some sad news. One of our son Bale's best friends at their church had a massive heart attack while playing racquetball last Saturday and passed away. He was only 52 years old and left behind a wife and two teenage daughters. Please keep the Greenwood family in your prayers. Life is so fragile, and we never know when the Lord will call us home.

On a brighter note, Reverend Miles and Sister Deseri are planning their wedding for October 16. They will have the ceremony at the church and a reception at Gage Park. It's such a blessing to see them doing things God's way, not the carnal way. They are a true testimony to living in obedience to the Lord.

How is your father and his new wife doing? We pray that his ministry is flourishing and that they are reaching the lost. Keep us in your prayers as well. And we want to thank you for the prayers you've offered for us. We received some good news recently—the doctors had suspected that Fred had Alzheimer's, but it turns out

The Federal Prison Sentence

he does not. Praise the Lord!

Well, my dear friend, keep the faith and continue to stand strong in the Lord. We trust that He has you right where He wants you, and we know He is using you mightily even in this season. May God bless and keep you always.

In Christ, *Pastor and Mother Holloman*

As I read through these letters, the prison walls fade for a moment. There's hope in each word, a reminder that even in the darkest of places, God's light shines through. Prison life may be harsh—the sights, the sounds, the violence—but through the noise, there is the soft, steady voice of God, breaking through the hardness of hearts. Each day presents an opportunity for transformation, and as God continues to work in and through these men, hope blossoms even here at Pekin.

July 19, 2010

God is so good! Today, I experienced something small but powerful. I went to the store here in Pekin, just a typical visit. But when I returned, I realized that they had given me an item without charging me for it. It was just $1.10—nothing big in the grand scheme of things. But Satan, always subtle, whispered in my ear, *"No one would know. It's only a dollar."*

But I know better, and I knew God was watching. At that moment, it wasn't just about the money. It was about my integrity, about whether I was going to honor God in the smallest of things. So I turned back around, went to the staff, and told them about the mistake. The staff member thanked me for my honesty, saying, *"Count*

Chapter Ten

it as a blessing." I smiled inside, knowing that $1.10 wasn't going to stand between me and God's blessings.

This moment reminded me of the subtle ways God speaks, testing us even in the smallest details of our lives. It's easy to overlook these little choices, but obedience matters. Today, I felt the Spirit moving, and I was obedient. As I reflect on my walk with God, I realize that there are areas in my life where I need to grow deeper:

- A hunger to know God more.

- A desire to understand the truth of His Word.

- An increased awareness of my own sinfulness.

- A quick response to sin, followed by genuine repentance.

- Joy, even in the midst of spiritual battles.

- Understanding that trials and temptations are opportunities for growth.

- Viewing service to God as an honor, not a burden.

- Seeing everything—good and bad—as coming from the Lord.

- Faith to ask God for bigger things.

- A strong desire to show and share God with others.

- An earnest commitment to give all my work to the Lord.

- An increased awareness of God in every area of my life.

- Prioritizing personal devotion as key to spiritual growth.

The journey is ongoing, and each day I see how much God is refining me. This place, as hard as it is, has been a training ground for my faith.

Dear Reverend Barbee,

What a joy it was for my husband and me to receive your letter! We want you to know that we pray for you every day, calling you by name and lifting up your prayer guide for the prisons. We praise God for how He is working in your life, molding you into the man He created you to be. His blessings are evident in your growth, and it's a joy to witness from afar.

We feel His blessings on us as well. His Word is our daily bread, always there to guide and comfort us. I have memorized several scriptures, which I pray daily for our family, our church, and our friends. There is such power in praying God's Word! It feels as though we are praying directly in line with His will when we speak His scriptures.

We are both doing well, especially now that the weather has cooled off. We've taken up walking two miles, six days a week, and it's been amazing to be out in God's creation, marveling at His handiwork. On top of that, we have exciting news—we became great-grandparents again last week! Our fifth great-granddaughter was born, and we expect another great-grandson in October. That will bring us to three boys and three girls among the

Chapter Ten

great-grandchildren. What a blessing! And by the end of the year, we will have welcomed our 18th grandchild—God is truly awesome.

The church is doing well, and there are some wonderful developments in the children's ministry. Praise the Lord! The family picnic and game day last month was a blast. The men's team finally won the tug-of-war; they were determined after losing last year. Everyone had such a good time. There was even a dunk tank, and all the ministers, including Elder Williams, got dunked at least once. It was a hot day, and I think they were secretly glad to cool off.

Next month will be Pastor and Mother Washington's anniversary, and we're already preparing for the celebration. Please pray that it will be an especially blessed day for them, full of love and appreciation. We can't wait for the day you come home! We love you and are constantly praying for you. Remember that you are cherished by us and the entire New Beginning Church family.

With love and prayers,
Pastor and Mother Holloman

As you read these letters, you can feel the vibrancy of life beyond the prison walls. The imagery of lush trees, joyful family gatherings, and the blossoming church community brings a sense of hope and excitement. Though the physical world of Pekin may feel confining, the spirit of these letters is expansive, filled with life, love, and the promise of God's work continuing both inside and out. The voices of loved ones reach across the miles, reassuring you that God's plans for you are still unfolding, even in this place.

September 26, 2010

Praise the Lord! God is so good. I've just received word that I'm moving downstairs into the residential drug and alcohol program unit here at Forrest City, Arkansas. This program is a 500-hour drug treatment course offered within the Federal Bureau of Prisons. Though the change comes with uncertainty, I can feel God's hand guiding me, reminding me that His plans are in motion.

October 21, 2010

I had an encounter where God spoke to me clearly. I was sitting across from a young man when the Lord revealed something so simple yet profound to me—this young man knew how to fix headphones, surely he could fix mine. It was a reminder that God is in the details. He challenged me to act in obedience, even in the smallest of things. It was as though God was asking, *"Do you hear Me now?"*

Initially, I hesitated in my obedience, delayed by my own doubts. But the Holy Spirit prompted me, nudging me out of my disobedience and into faithful action. By stepping out in faith, I'm learning to trust that God's call is constant, even in moments that seem insignificant. I've asked the Lord to keep working on me, on me, and through me. I want to be the man He created me to be, fully surrendered to His will.

Forrest City brings its own challenges—the spirit of competition and judgmentalism is present here. But I'm reminded that as members of the body of Christ, we are called to be more than just individuals striving for per-

Chapter Ten

sonal gain. My prayer is that I can be a light, an example of what God wants the church to be here, even in a place like this.

October 11, 2010

Dear Reverend Barbee,

What a blessing it was to receive your letter! Pastor Holloman and I continue to pray for you daily, and it fills our hearts with joy to hear how the Lord is using you for His purpose, even in these trying circumstances. We are praying that an opening will become available soon in the drug program, and we eagerly await the day you return to Kansas.

Both Pastor and I are doing well, and we praise the Master for granting us good health. This month is Pastor Appreciation Month, and we've been blessed with a full calendar of activities. On Saturday, we had an appreciation brunch for the associate preachers and their wives—it was a beautiful event, and the ladies put on a wonderful meal and program. Yesterday, one of the associate pastors preached a powerful message. What a blessing it is to have such a strong group of men serving the Lord at New Beginning Church.

We pray that one day, you too will return to serve in that capacity. We understand that there will be a period of restoration, but that's to be expected. Your gifts and calling are undeniable, and we look forward to the day when you can minister again.

Please keep Mother Washington in your prayers, as she continues to battle health issues. We also ask for your prayers for Reverend Miles and Desiree, who are getting

The Federal Prison Sentence

married this Saturday. It promises to be a joyous occasion, with a capacity crowd expected. Desiree's mother, Carolyn, has been here for a few weeks, helping with preparations to ensure the wedding is a true blessing.

We are praying for their union, that it will be centered in God's will and that their marriage will reflect His love in every way. God bless you, Reverend Barbee. Know that we continue to pray for you and trust that God's hand is upon your life.

With love and prayers,
Mother Holloman

The letters I received speak of God's unwavering presence, even in the midst of my life's test. As I, Reverend Barbee, transitioned into the drug program, it's clear that my journey is marked by obedience and faith. Even in the face of temptation, competition, and judgment, I continued to seek God's will in all things. The support from his church family, coupled with the consistent encouragement from loved ones like Mother Holloman, serves as a reminder that the call of God never leaves us, even when we travel off the intended path set for our lives. God can redeem our time. The words exchanged between these letters thus far are not just letters—they are lifelines of hope, a powerful testimony of faith, and an ever-present reminder that God's work continues in the lives of His people.

October 29, 2020.

Thank you, Lord! Today marked my third day here in the drug unit—a new reality, a different world, but

Chapter Ten

Your Word reminds me that You will never leave me nor forsake me. In the quiet moments of reflection, I feel Your presence, and I hold onto that promise. God, I thank You for guiding me through this transition, even as my spirit adjusts to this place.

Tonight, something incredible happened. I went down to the laundry room to wash my clothes, a simple task, but You, Lord, turned it into something much greater. As I stood in line, waiting my turn, I saw a young man named James. He was working at the ironing board, lost in thought, his expression distant yet calm. I could feel something familiar, something spiritual about him. We started talking, our conversation was easy and natural, and it wasn't long before I discovered that James, too, is a believer in Christ.

It felt almost surreal—like when Jesus met the woman at the well. Here I was, standing in the laundry room of a federal prison, meeting another believer, not at a church, not at a Bible study, but by the ironing board of all places. It was as if You had orchestrated this encounter, Lord, shining Your light even in this unlikely setting. We were in a place of darkness, surrounded by concrete walls and steel bars, yet You manifested Your presence between two strangers, two believers.

As we continued talking, I felt Your Spirit move. I shared my testimony—how I had heard Your voice, Lord, and how obedience to You had transformed my life, even amidst all the chaos and challenges. It was a moment of vulnerability, but also one of deep connection. And then, right there in the middle of that laundry room, we prayed together. We thanked You, Lord, for keeping us, for being our light in this place of shadows.

The Federal Prison Sentence

In that moment, You revealed six powerful truths to me:

- Confidence in my calling—despite where I am, I know You've chosen me for a purpose.

- Strength in adversity—this place is tough, but I feel Your strength within me.

- Balance in godly character—You're refining me, teaching me how to carry myself in a way that reflects Your heart.

- Faith in the face of violence—this environment can be harsh, but I trust You to protect me.

- Persistence in prayer—prayer is my lifeline, my constant connection to You.

- Consistency in my praise—no matter what, I will continue to worship You, Lord.

Who would have thought that in a federal prison laundry room, I would find fellowship, prayer, and Your overwhelming light? Only You could orchestrate such a moment, Lord. You are here with me, even in the most unexpected place. And for that, I am forever grateful.

Amen.

Chapter Ten

Chapter ELEVEN

THE TURNING POINT: REDEMPTION IN PRISON

There were several pivotal moments in my life that sparked my redemption journey and revealed a pattern forming in my heart to be more like Christ.

October 30, 2010

As I reflect today, God is showing me something profound. Life is a journey of overcoming and pushing forward—pressing into Jesus and pushing aside every obstacle while pursuing Him. It's a constant struggle, but with each step, stability releases ability. My gifts, though given, are not enough. It's my character that needs development. I hear God reminding me that sight, right, and might are essential, but I must fight for them. A good idea may come and go, but a God ideal always manifests. This is why I need to be consistent and persistent in

Chapter Eleven

everything I do.

God has challenged me to examine the following areas in my life where I need to grow and develop consistency in order to become more Christlike.

- **I need to be available**—to God, to others, to the moments where He speaks or leads.

- **I need to be held accountable**–allowing trusted people to hold me to the standard God sets.

- **I need to be dependable** – showing up, doing what I say I will, reflecting God's steadfastness.

- **I must be generous in my giving** – not just money, but time, attention, love, and forgiveness.

- **I must be honest** – in every word and action, aligning with truth.

- **I must be loyal** – standing firm in my faith, my relationships, and in my commitments.

- **I must be pure and holy**–- living set apart, resisting temptation, and seeking righteousness.

- **I must be sensitive**—to God's Spirit, to the needs of others, and to the moments when He moves.

- **I must be transparent**—open, and vulnerable, allowing others to see the real me, as God sees me.

The Turning Point: Redemption in Prison

November 1, 2010

As I reflect on the lessons God has been teaching me, I realize how much I have learned during this time.

- **I have learned to be thankful** for my spiritual family—those who stand by me in prayer and encouragement.

- **I have learned that prayer works**—in ways I didn't always understand before. God moves through prayer, even in the darkest places.

- **I have learned that trouble can lead to victory**—that it isn't something to be feared but embraced as part of God's plan for growth.

- **I have learned not to fear death**—knowing that my eternity is secure in Christ, who gives me peace.

- **I have learned that suffering is not always the result of sin**—sometimes it is part of God's refinement process.

- **I have learned to think the thoughts of Christ**—aligning my mind with His Word and His will.

- **I have learned that God works through me**—that despite my past and my failures, He is using me now.

- **I have learned not to risk the things that matter**—to hold fast to the things of eternal value.

Chapter Eleven

- **I have learned that life is best when I know that God is personally intimate in my life**—this relationship with Him is everything.

- **I have learned not to quit**—even when it's hard, I can press on.

- **I have learned not to worry**—God is in control, even when I am not.

- **I have learned to think right**—to focus on the things that are true, noble, right, and pure.

- **I have learned to be content**—in every circumstance, knowing that God is my source.

- **I have learned that I can do all things through Christ who strengthens me**—there is no limit to what God can do through me.

- **I have learned that Jesus Christ is the only source of my supply**—in Him, I have everything I need.

November 6, 2010

I received a letter from Mother Hollomon today. It was uplifting for her to hear that I'll be getting into the drug program soon—another step on this journey God is leading me through. Reverend Barbee, as she calls me, "My family and I are praying for you every day, and we praise God for how He is working in your life," is what the letter said back to me. It was the right kind of encouragement when I needed it most.

They shared news from home—the Jayhawks are

doing well, which brought a smile to my face. How I miss the simple joys of life outside, like watching a game or celebrating a friend's wedding. It's the small things like that which remind me of God's goodness, even in the midst of hardship. Reverend Barbee closed the letter with encouragement, reminding me to stay strong in my walk with the Lord.

November 21, 2010

This is another day the Lord has made, and I will rejoice in it! God is so good. A few days ago, I sat down with another inmate named PB from Florida. He challenged me in a way that has stuck with me. He looked at me and said, "Barbee, your words are powerful."

He explained that as we sat in group therapy, he noticed how the others listened when I spoke, how they hung onto every word. PB's encouragement sparked something in me. He suggested that perhaps I am called to become a motivational speaker—to use my time here to groom this gift for God's glory.

That hit me hard. Could this be my purpose in all this? Could God be shaping me to speak life and hope into others? I realize now that I need to pray, to ask God for His guidance, to show me how His will can be done through me at this time in my life.

My prayer is simple: **Lord, break me down until there is no more of me left. Let me decrease so that You may increase in me. Keep my vision sharp and my focus clear, as Genesis 50:20 says, "What Satan meant for evil, You, God, meant for good."**

I said within my heart, This imprisonment, this

Chapter Eleven

season of my life—it's all for Your glory. I know now that the only way out is through You, Lord. My addiction was my bondage, my Pharaoh. But just as You freed the Israelites, You are freeing me, not just to liberate me, but so I can worship You fully.

I must move deeper into worship because real worship opens another world—one where I can experience more of You, God. In worship, I leave behind my Pharaoh, and the unmovable obstacles in my life are moved through praise. Keep me in this place, Lord, seeking more of You. Amen.

The spiritual reflections of December 2010 through January 2011 mark a profound journey of revelation, humility, and leadership for me. On December 5, I was filled with the awareness of God's purpose and influence in my life, realizing that leadership isn't just a title, but the ability to be a light for others, a living example of Christ's presence. I finally surrendered to the idea that I'm not in control, but that God is, which shows a deep level of faith and spiritual maturity. The concept of "letting God be God" suggests that I am learning to step aside and allow His will to manifest fully, trusting in His divine plan for my life.

The confirmation that I am called to lead, not just within the body of Christ but in all areas of life, seems to have shifted my perception of influence. Leadership to me meant being a living testimony—allowing Christ in me to be seen by others, which is a powerful revelation. I recognized the importance of being comfortable not only in my identity but also in my divine purpose, acknowledging that my role was to let God's glory shine through me..

The Turning Point: Redemption in Prison

December 22

I continued to reflect on God's faithfulness and the importance of walking in truth. This time, the test came through a counselor who doubted my financial truth. They didn't think I would pay my fines, but it was in my heart to do it. But I remained steadfast in your commitment to honesty, knowing that the truth would ultimately prevail. It was an important moment of trust, a reminder that even when people don't believe you, God's plans and your faithfulness will overcome obstacles. The interview for the residential drug and alcohol program seemed to be a breakthrough moment for you, knowing that God had orchestrated the timing perfectly to align with His plan.

January 16, 201

The theme of surrendering to God's will became more pronounced. I faced delays and frustrations, but instead of yielding to disappointment, you recognized it as part of God's plan for your growth. The comment made by someone in your unit, referring to you as "a real Christian," shows the fruit of your commitment to living authentically. I have become a beacon of faith within that environment, and people are noticing.

My interactions with others, like Mr. Kelly considering leaving the program or Jr. seeking understanding of Psalms 19, reveal how your influence extended beyond words—it became about actions, about being present in a way that mirrored the heart of Christ. These moments speak to the idea that people are looking not just for sermons to listen to but for sermons to witness in the lives of others. I understood that to be filled with the Holy

Chapter Eleven

Spirit, to decrease in your own desires so that Christ could increase in you, was the ultimate calling.

This time seems to have been one of intense spiritual growth, where your faith was not only tested but also refined. Every situation, every interaction, carried a deeper spiritual significance as you embraced the transformational power of God's love and grace.

January 22, 2011:

The cold steel of prison life settled in as just another day when the 3 o'clock yard recall rang through the unit. I made my way back inside, the chill of winter still clinging to my coat as I draped it over the bunk. As I sat down, something profound stirred in me—the unmistakable voice of the Holy Spirit. *Call home.* It was as clear as if someone had whispered it in my ear.

I hesitated for a second, then obeyed. I headed for the phone, dialing with a mix of anticipation and unease. Mrs. Helen answered. Our conversation was brief, but there was a warmth in her voice. When she handed the phone to Dad, I felt a sense of peace. His voice, filled with wisdom, said, "God's timing is always right on time." It struck me. And then I heard them—Brian and Vicki were both there, ready to talk. I hadn't expected it, but that's the thing with God. It's not just about hearing His voice; it's about being obedient when He calls; that obedience opens doors.

I thanked God for guiding me in that moment, for reminding me that He's always in control, even in the smallest things.

January 22, 2011 (Later):

The Turning Point: Redemption in Prison

It's strange how quickly prison can change from mundane to meaningful. This past week, I saw God moving in ways that left me awestruck. On Tuesday, the secretary called my name several times, but I was over at the chapel, working. When I finally returned to the unit, the buzz was immediate. Inmates came up to me one after another—*You need to see your case manager.*

I knew something was stirring. When I arrived, she handed me a legal letter. My heart pounded in my chest. *Could this be about the new crack law?* I'd been studying it, hoping, praying that it might benefit me. The letter was from the Kansas Public Defender's Office. They told me my case was open and they were waiting for the Sentencing Commission to make changes to the guidelines. The letter hinted at hope—*something could happen within 90 days.* I could be on my way home.

Lord, I surrender to Your timing. Whatever happens, it's in Your hands.

January 22, 2011 (Evening):

In the thick of prison life, it's easy to become hardened, but God keeps showing me how to stay soft, how to remain open to His guidance. Just yesterday, a brother named Mr. Sims received devastating news—his father had passed. I knew his father had been ill, but nothing prepares you for that kind of loss. I felt the nudge of the Holy Spirit to go to him, to pray with him. We stood there, two men surrounded by the walls of this place, but at that moment, those walls didn't matter. What mattered was God using me to be there for someone else.

January 23, 2011:

Chapter Eleven

The truth is, God isn't punishing me, and He hasn't forgotten me. I remind myself of that as the days tick by, one after another. Instead, He's holding me—steadying me—through every trial.

February 2, 2011:

Today was the last day of a program in the chapel, and God was moving. Chaplain Rains pulled me aside and asked me to take on a new role—to leave my orderly job and work in the chapel office. It was confirmation of something I've known for a while—*God makes room for our gifts.* One of mine is leadership and administration, and now, even behind bars, He's giving me a platform to use those gifts.

The enemy doesn't like this, though. I feel the pushback, the pressure. But I'm learning that the battle is already won. Jesus secured the victory. My job is just to stay faithful. As I stood there, Chaplain Rains looked me in the eye and asked about the rumors, the gossip circulating in the prison. I told her plainly, "Talk doesn't affect me anymore." People talked about me when I was on crack, so why should it bother me now as I serve the Lord?

I don't know everything God is doing in my life, but I know He's at work. I'm thankful and grateful for that. *Not my will, but Yours be done, Lord.*

February 11, 2011:

This week, I've had to remind myself constantly—*God is in control.* Tuesday night's service was a revealing one. I stood there, emceeing the service, as men like Sam, Bruce, and Newborn expressed one thing with their

The Turning Point: Redemption in Prison

words—*I don't need a title or position.* But their actions said otherwise. I could see the struggle in their hearts, the desire for recognition. And I understood it because they, like me, have served long sentences. They've been stripped of their identities, and sometimes, titles seem like a way to reclaim them.

But God's been teaching me what ministry really is—it's not about the spotlight; it's about service. It's about being broken, letting God use the pieces to rebuild something beautiful. I can sense the tension in the spiritual realm as well as the physical. It feels like after every storm, there's a cleanup, and right now, God is cleaning house. Both in the church and in my heart, He is making rounds.

I've learned to expect persecution. I've learned to expect people to talk about me. But I won't let that stop me from doing what God has called me to do. Lord, I'm praying for a deeper relationship with You. Break me down again if You have to, because I know You can use the broken pieces.

Help me to be the father You want me to be to my children—Stephen Anthony, Sherell Lynn, and Latasha Marie. Guide my steps, Lord, because I know they're watching. Every day is a step closer to You.

February 19, 2011:

As I sit in my cell, the silence around me amplifies my thoughts, bouncing off the cold, hard walls. I take out Reverend Barbee's letter and read it slowly, savoring every word. It's a reminder that even behind bars, God's work in my life continues. Reverend Barbee wrote with such faith and conviction, confirming that God is answering the

Chapter Eleven

prayers of so many on my behalf. His words were more than just encouragement—they were an affirmation of the journey I'm on.

The verse he included, Romans 11:29—*the gifts and calling of God are irrevocable*—stirs something deep inside me. The weight of it settles over me like a blanket of hope. Even though I'm here in this cell, isolated and separated from the world, I know my gifts are still mine, and the calling God placed on my life has not been snatched away by these circumstances.

I think about what Reverend Barbee said: *You are blooming where God has planted you.* That simple phrase shifts my perspective. I'm not here to just endure this time; I'm here to grow, to flourish in a place where it seems impossible. The ground beneath me may feel barren, but God has a way of bringing life out of dry places.

February 27, 2011:

The clamor of prison life doesn't stop. Inmates yell across the halls, some trying to pass time, others just making noise to fill the void. But in the midst of all the distractions, I find moments of clarity. Today, I'm reflecting on what it truly means to *deny myself and serve the Lord.*

It's not easy to hear people talk badly about me, but it's strange—I've started to rejoice when I hear it. Not because I enjoy it, but because it reminds me that I'm walking in truth. This journey has been about learning to submit to authority—not just the authority over me in prison, but ultimately, God's authority. Every day I choose obedience, I feel a little more of His peace settle

The Turning Point: Redemption in Prison

over me.

I think about my conversation with Brother Wen earlier today. He shared with me how my presence in the office has brought some stability to the religious department. His words were humbling, but also affirming. He noticed how I interact with people of all races—whites, blacks, Latinos—there are no boundaries. That brought back something Dad always told me: *You can impress people from a distance, but to make an impact, you have to get up close.*

In prison, getting close to people isn't easy. Trust is a commodity more rare than gold here. But I've tried to live by that principle—being up close with others, listening to them, understanding their stories. It's the only way to truly make an impact.

I received a letter today. It was from Marie, my ex-wife. I hadn't heard from her in a long time, and to be honest, I didn't know what to expect when I wrote her asking for forgiveness. When I opened her letter, my heart was racing. She told me she had forgiven me a long time ago, and I felt a weight lift off my shoulders. But then she shared something that sent me reeling—news about our son, Stephen. His behavior has spiraled out of control. He's using drugs, and now his girlfriend is pregnant.

As I read her words, I could feel the guilt closing in on me. My absence from his life has taken a toll. I wasn't there to guide him when he needed me most. How did things go so wrong? But then, Brother Al reminded me of something. He told me this attack on my family is confirmation that I'm walking in God's will. If I weren't,

Chapter Eleven

Satan wouldn't be trying so hard to bring me down through my family.

His words didn't take away the pain, but they gave me perspective. I can't just sit here and worry; I need to fight in the only way I know how—through prayer. I began to pray with a new intensity, claiming God's protection over my son. *The blood of Jesus is placed over my family.* I said it again and again, praying that every attack of the enemy would be thwarted.

This battle isn't just mine—it's the Lord's. And while I may not be able to be there for Steven physically, I know God is. He can go where I cannot. So I continue to pray, believing that even in the midst of this storm, God is working. I cling to the hope that just as He's working on me, He's working on my family, too.

MARCH 2011

My reflection from March 2011 speaks volumes about the power of faith, honesty, and community. It shows how even in a difficult situation, like being in prison, I found meaning and saw God's provision in unexpected ways, such as when others provided for me by giving me something as simple as coffee. This small but profound experience reinforced my belief in Ephesians 3:20, that God can do abundantly more than we imagine. My openness with the community, even in moments of frustration, led to unexpected blessings. This honesty, coupled with my faith, allowed me to witness how God was working in the hearts of those around me, demonstrating His care and provision.

My prayer with Chaplain Rain also highlights the

importance of ministering to others, especially those who are often overlooked. My compassion toward her and her family, and the act of praying for her, is a beautiful testament to my mission of service, encouragement, and empowerment. Even in a challenging environment, I was fulfilling my personal mission statement by helping others and living out my purpose.

The idea that I "refuse to waste this prison time" is a powerful declaration of my resilience and commitment to growth. I acknowledge my past choices, but I also show that I was using this time to build my character and serve my community. I believe that my reflections can be deeply inspiring and show how God's presence can transform any situation into an opportunity for growth, service, and deepening faith.

March 10, 2011

Reflection on the Shakedown and God's Provision:

During a **unit shakedown**, they **confiscated** my coffee, not as a personal attack, but as a consequence of my past behaviors that led to prison. Initially, I was **angry**, but I chose to **share my frustration** with the community, being open and honest. That act of transparency led me to witness the **glory of God** in action.

Suddenly, men whom I normally talk to, and even those I don't, started **approaching me** and **giving me bags of coffee**. I would **sit in my cube**, and out of nowhere, coffee would **appear under my bunk** or even **in my pocket**. God's provision showed up in the most unexpected ways, and others can demonstrate their faith by pouring into me. I couldn't help but recall Ephe-

Chapter Eleven

sians 3:20, realizing that God is able to do **abundantly more than I could ever imagine**. Each coffee gift was a tangible reminder that He provides for our needs, often beyond our expectations.

March 16, 2011

Sherell's Birthday and Continuing Signs of God's Favor:

Yesterday was Sherell's 15th birthday, and I **tried to call** her to speak with her, but the number was **disconnected**. For a moment, I was **disheartened**, but I quickly turned back to the community and chose to continue to **reflect on how God provides**. Once again, I experienced the same overwhelming sense of grace—men were still **offering me coffee** without me asking, and I drank the coffee and sent up prayers on behalf of my daughter. God continued the testament of his goodness and ability to fulfill my needs beyond what I anticipated.

In another moment of clarity, the Holy Spirit **prompted me** to go pray with Chaplain Rain. I felt an undeniable sense of obedience, so I approached her, and we **prayed together** for her sick parents, her daughter Emily, and her chaplaincy work. Afterward, she **sat with me quietly**, visibly moved. She told me that, in all her years at Forest City, only three people had ever **prayed for her**. This was a powerful moment of empathy, reminding me how often we forget that even those who serve others need **care and prayer** for themselves.

Chapter TWELVE

A NEW MISSION: FROM PRISONER TO PURPOSE

March 17, 2011

Turning Prison Time into Purpose:

Today, I had a profound realization: though I **hate being in prison**, I absolutely **refuse to waste** this time. I understand that the choices I made led me here, but I can still **learn and grow** from my experiences, and that learning comes from **the company I keep**—my community. This moment deepened my sense of responsibility to build and **strengthen my character**, as well as to stay true to my convictions.

I've defined my **personal mission statement**: **To serve, to help, to encourage, and to empower**. By doing these things each day, I'm inspired to live with purpose. Part of that purpose is to continue **shedding light** on others, offering hope where it's needed, and being the hands and feet of God's love.

In all of these moments, you're actively engaging with the world around you. Whether it's **choosing to share** your frustrations, **being obedient to pray** for someone else, or **deciding not to waste** your time in a difficult place, you consistently **take action** that aligns with your faith. Each instance is a testament to how God's truth not only sets you free but also fills your life with meaning and abundance.

March 25, 2011

As I sit here in my prison cell, the gray walls around me feel closer than ever, yet your letter, Reverend Barbee, is like a breath of fresh air. It's always good to hear about what the Lord is doing outside these bars. The Ministry for the King, as you said, is filled with challenges, but it's exciting to know that even though we face trials, God is ever present, moving in our lives.

You shared about Pastor Holloman, and I can feel the weight of his struggle with memory loss. I picture him still standing at the pulpit, his voice steady as he preaches, though time is slowly claiming his sharpness. You are celebrating your church's anniversary of thirteen years, you said? That's powerful, a true testament to faith and perseverance. I can almost see the smiles, the worship, the fellowship as your congregation comes together to celebrate. Meanwhile, I sit here in the quiet of my cell, but I'm celebrating with you in spirit.

Mother Holloman's health weighs heavily on my heart as well. Her struggle with pain management reminds me of how fragile our bodies are, but the apparatus you mentioned—something about a device under the skin—gives me hope that relief is possible. I'll be keeping her in my prayers.

Kansas Prayer Breakfast... I can almost hear the music in my head as I read your words. I imagine the room filled with people lifting up their voices in praise. The new governor being there is a reminder that, even in political arenas, God's work continues, and we are encouraged to keep standing firm in our faith.

I caught a brief smile when you mentioned KU and K-State's seasons. My mind drifts back to times when I would watch basketball with excitement. The world out there is still moving, while here, time moves a little differently. But I hold on to hope, Reverend, knowing that God has a plan even for me behind these bars.

March 26, 2011

Today, I sit with a deeper sense of gratitude. **Thank you, Lord,** for this week, this day, and this journey. It's been an interesting week, no doubt. Thursday marked a pivotal moment: I was **officially enrolled in the residential drug and alcohol program**. This means that by December 2011, I'll have graduated, and by January 2012, I'll finally be home. The thought of freedom feels surreal, but it's a hope I hold onto with everything I've got.

Last week, I watched as the last group of men graduated and left. Some of them came up to me, thanking me for my words of encouragement. One young man from Florida—a seeker of truth—stood out to me. I re-

Chapter Twelve

member the conversations we had, and I told him plainly, "I wasn't trying to impress you, just trying to make an impact." Sometimes, all we can do is show people Jesus, through our words, our actions, and how we live our lives, even in the most difficult places.

I moved to a new cubicle this week, and my new cellmate, Eric Walker, and I have already had a couple of deep conversations. I know God is about relationships—He builds us up through the connections we make with others. With Eric, I realize that for any relationship to grow, I have to **invest** in it. God is teaching me that it's not just about me. If I want to get something out of these relationships, I need to give of myself first. In that giving, I find freedom. **God lift me up** to set me free, even here.

April 1, 2011

I woke up this morning with the weight of my flesh heavy on me. **There is no good thing in my flesh**, Lord, and I know that I must die to myself daily if I want to live for You. I want to be **used by You**, not just today, but for the rest of my life. I understand that trials will come, that I will face tests and temptations. But I also know my position in Christ. In my **flesh**, I cannot, but in Christ's **resurrection**, I can.

It's easy to focus on the chains, the walls, the mistakes that landed me here. But I've learned not to focus on my **condition**, but on my **position** in Christ. Living a **resurrected life** means living with hope, purpose, and the knowledge that through Christ, I've already been set free, even before I walk out of these gates.

A New Mission: From Prisoner to Purpose

In the quiet of this cell, I pray and I reflect. It's not about the place I'm in—it's about where I stand in Christ. This is my resurrection, and I'm determined to live it out, every day, even here.

I know God is at work in our lives, and He is using every situation, no matter how challenging, for His glory. Here are the key points that stand out from my Bible studies and personal time with God:

- **God Speaks and Leads Through You**: In the April 10th letter, I talk about hearing God's voice and being obedient to it. Whether it's giving a book to a brother in need or blessing someone else with knowledge, I was acting as an instrument of God's will. This highlights your role as a vessel for God's voice and provision in others' lives. **Listening to God's voice** and obeying His promptings allows me to bless others, showing how deeply He is involved in my day-to-day decisions.

- **Personal Growth and Leadership**: In the April 16th letter, there's a reflection on how God is using me as a leader, not just in ministry but in life. I recognize that while others may perceive me as "preachy," I am learning to balance my role with humility and discernment. I was seeing the fruits of the Spirit within me—**boldness, authority, and Christ's life**—as I embrace your identity in Him. There's a growing understanding of who I am and how to lead those around me without compromising my faith.

- **Trials Turned to Good**: I acknowledge that what

Chapter Twelve

Satan intended for harm, God is turning into good (April 16). The challenges I face, such as feedback on how I come across to others, are refining me. God is using even the difficult moments to shape me into a stronger, more discerning leader. This is a powerful reminder that every trial is an opportunity for growth and transformation in God's hands.

- **The Call to Serve**: Throughout these letters, there is an underlying theme of **service**. Whether it's within my prison community or back home in Kansas, there's a strong sense of being called to help, support, and encourage others. The letter from May 17 reflects the **needs of my home community** and their eagerness for my return. They pray for me and wait for the moment when I can come back and continue the ministry that they know I am destined for. This underscores the importance of my role in the lives of others, both near and far.

- **Hope and Anticipation for Freedom**: The prayers and updates from the May 17 letter remind me that many are eagerly waiting for my return, hoping for me to come back and lead. There is an anticipation for the next chapter of my life, not just for me but for the people who look to me for guidance. This affirms the **significance of my impact** and how my journey, even through hardship, is preparing me for greater things outside of prison.

Main Message: God is using my circumstances to mold me into the leader and servant He has called me to be. Through obedience, personal reflection, and service, I am becoming a vessel for His glory, even in the most unlikely places. I continue to listen, grow, and trust that every step is part of His divine plan for my life.

April 10, 2011

I'm sitting on my bunk in the prison cell with a worn Bible beside me. The sounds of prison life hum around me—men playing cards, others walking by—but at this moment, I'm reflecting deeply. There's been this book on Bible doctrine sitting in the chapel for over two months, and every time I saw it, something inside me stirred. It felt like a battle within—part of me wanted to grab it for myself, dive into its wisdom. But something held me back. I couldn't take it. Not yet.

Then yesterday, I ran into a brother. He was working on several papers, studying different doctrines. It clicked. **This** was why I hadn't taken the book. The Spirit was leading me. The next morning, I walked into the chapel, grabbed the book, and handed it to him. His face lit up, his joy was undeniable. The book was meant for him, not me. That's when I felt it again—that **whisper of God**, directing me.

Later that afternoon, I came across another book, *The Power of Praise* by Merle Crothers. This time, I heard God clearly, almost like He was standing next to me: **Hold onto the book. I'll tell you who it's for.** And so, I did. It wasn't long before Brother Mike walked into the library. We started talking, fellowshipping. I mentioned Crothers' name, and Mike's eyes widened—he'd been looking for this book. Once again, the Spirit had led me to bless someone else.

Chapter Twelve

These moments remind me of something important: God is speaking, always. The question is, **are we listening?** My prayer is that I continue to die to myself daily, to my own desires, and instead listen to what the Spirit says. I want to lead—not for my sake, but for the sake of others. **God, make me the leader this community needs.**

April 16, 2011

Today, sitting in the drug unit at Forrest City, Arkansas, I'm filled with awe at how **God can turn everything around for good**. Just days ago, feedback from the community hit me hard—they said I came across as "preachy" or "churchy." At first, I felt defensive. I'm a licensed and ordained minister, for heaven's sake! But then I realized: **this was a teaching moment**.

Yesterday, I stood up in front of the community. I could've been defensive, but instead, I shared openly. I told them who I am, my role, my journey. But here's the thing—**I didn't preach, I didn't quote scripture**. I simply let my words speak life. I didn't hide the fact that Christ lives in me, that the words I speak are filled with light and conviction because of Him.

The real challenge is discernment. The enemy is always lurking, trying to twist things, but I walk in the power and authority that Christ has given me. **I know who I am**. And I know that as God increases in me, I must continue to decrease. There are men around me—hurt, lost, broken. And God is calling me to encourage them, to show them the love of Christ, not just through words but through action.

A New Mission: From Prisoner to Purpose

May 3, 2011

A letter came today from Pastor and Mother Holloman. As I read it, I felt the distance between us shrink. They're waiting for me in Kansas. The congregation is praying for my return. It's been a long journey, but their words remind me of **the impact I've had and the people still counting on me**.

The church is growing—twenty kids, most Sundays. The youth, the children—they're being guided by Brother Jason and Sister Dorothy. There's still so much to be done, and they're waiting for me to come home to help pass the baton to the next generation. Pastor and Mother Washington have been struggling with health issues, and she's facing surgery on her back. It's a reminder of the fragility of life, of the **faithfulness that keeps us all going**.

They pray for me, for the day I'll walk through those doors again, ready to lead, ready to take up where I left off. Until then, all I can do is continue to grow, continue to learn from the Spirit, and prepare for the work God has ahead for me.

As I sit here in this cell, reading these letters and reflecting on the Spirit's voice, I realize something: God is not bound by these walls. His work, His will, continues both inside and outside of this place. There's leadership He's calling me to, both here and out in the world. But before I can lead others, I have to let Him lead me.

Every day, I'm learning to **listen more, to die to myself, and to trust God's timing**

Chapter Twelve

. It's not easy. Sometimes it feels like these walls are closing in, but the truth is, God is bigger than this place. He's preparing me for something greater, something beyond these bars.

As I read these letters, I feel both the weight of responsibility and the incredible peace that comes from knowing that **God is in control**. All I need to do is stay faithful, keep listening, and let Him use me wherever I am.

May 4, 2011

It's a new day, but today feels different. There's a weight pressing on my spirit, a sense that **I need to surrender more deeply to the Lord**. Yesterday's prayers, yesterday's revelations—they were good for that day, but they're not enough to carry me through today. I feel the emptiness that comes when you try to rely on yesterday's manna to fill today's hunger. **I need fresh bread from heaven today**.

The truth hits me: **time with God must be a daily priority**. I can feel Him molding and shaping me into His image, but that process requires me to be fully present with Him every day. It's like a potter with clay—you can't walk away from the wheel and expect the masterpiece to form on its own. I've had the heart to serve Him, but I realize now I need to **walk more closely with His Spirit**, to be filled anew each morning.

Here, in this prison, the faces around me tell stories. The men here wear their history, their pain, and their guilt in their expressions and actions. I can see what's in their hearts just by the way they carry themselves—their

A New Mission: From Prisoner to Purpose

words, their choices. But I'm no different. **Lord, help me discern the good from the evil, expose my enemies**, so that even in this dark place, I can reflect You. **Let them see Jesus in me**, not my flaws, not my mistakes.

Saturday night stands out in my mind. I sat with a young man, hardened by life, shaped by the streets. He's deep in gang life—it's all he's ever known. As we talked, I could see the cracks in his armor. He confessed something that has weighed heavily on his soul: **he sold drugs to his own mother**. The guilt in his eyes was unmistakable. He looked at me, seeking some form of redemption, some way to wash away the stain of what he had done.

I told him what I knew to be true: **he needs to forgive himself, and God will forgive him**. I saw relief flicker across his face as I spoke. He admitted that he felt God tugging on him, pulling him out of the darkness. **I encouraged him to lean into that tug**. God tugged on me, too, once. And I tugged back. **Amen.**

May 12, 2011

I woke up this morning thanking God for who He is in my life. **What a week it has been**. Monday came with a blessing—Dad and Brian came to visit me. Seeing them brought life into this cold place. It was more than just a visit; it was a reminder that **God is still taking care of my family**. We sat together, and they filled me in on what's been happening back home. Dad, he's as strong as ever, unshakable. At 73 years old, he's still moving, still fighting, still standing tall. It reminds me of the rock he's always been in my life.

There's a part of me that aches to not be out there,

Chapter Twelve

supporting him, supporting the family, and the ministry. I miss it all, and I pray that the Lord will release me from here soon, so I can be there when they need me most. I need to be there to **help carry the mantle** that's being passed down.

I received a letter this week from **Mother Holloman**, and her words brought both joy and heaviness. She told me things are going well at New Beginning Church in Topeka, but her words carried a deeper message—**the elders are passing the mantle to us, the younger generation**. It's a weight I feel on my shoulders now more than ever. The work they've done, the foundation they've built—it's up to us to carry it forward.

I can't help but think about the future. **Where will I go when I get out of here?** What does the Lord have planned for me? I hear Mother Holloman's words in my head, and I know the responsibility that's waiting for me. The younger generation has to take up the work to continue building on what the elders started. But even as I contemplate my release, my thoughts are also here, with the men around me. **The church inside this prison is divided**, torn apart by petty differences and egos; it's heartbreaking.

I realize that if there is to be any unity, any hope for the church here, it must start with me. I have to be willing to **die to myself**, to let go of my will, my wants, and my desires. Only then can **God's will be done**. Only then can unity begin to manifest. As I reflect, I can hear the words echo in my spirit: **Die, die, die—to my will, my wants, and my desires.**

Lord, let Your will be done, here in this place and in

A New Mission: From Prisoner to Purpose

my life. **I surrender to You once again.**

May 17, 2011

Dear Reverend Barbee,

We've been praying for your safe return to Kansas, and we hope it will be soon. We've become accustomed to the prayer leader you sent for us each day, and he's doing a wonderful job keeping our spirits lifted. Things are going well at New Beginning Church. The children and youth programs are thriving, and we've had as many as 20 young ones joining us on most Sundays. Brother Jason and Sister Dorothy Roberts have been working with the youth, and they've been such a blessing to the church.

Please keep Pastor and Mother Washington in your prayers. They've both been struggling with their health lately, and Mother Washington may need surgery on her back. She's in terrible pain most of the time. We're also asking for your prayers for my husband, who will be undergoing hernia surgery in June. As you know, many of our older members are growing more dependent on the younger generation to step in and take over. We need you so much here, Reverend Barbee, to help pass the baton on.

Reverend Miles recently lost his job with the city bus company, but he's now driving a tour bus, and we hope he will find stability there. Please also pray for Reverend Williams, who retired from the city this year and is in need of income.

We're looking forward to heading to Dallas in July for our granddaughter's wedding. It should be a beautiful

Chapter Twelve

time for the family to come together, and we'll be sure to keep you in our prayers while we're there. We truly hope this letter finds you well and that we hear some good news about your return soon.

With love and blessings,
Pastor and Mother Holloman

June 4, 2011

Thank you, Lord, for being the constant guide and the Lord of my life. Today, I can truly say that I am learning more and more about what it means to have faith in You in every aspect of my journey. As I sit here in cell number 154 at the Federal Correctional Institution in Forrest City, I reflect on the joy that fills my heart, a joy that can only come from You. My life is firmly in Your hands, and I am beginning to see Your plans and purposes manifest in my life in ways I couldn't have imagined.

I used to long to witness the supernatural, to see miraculous signs. But now, I'm beginning to understand that true faith lies in the simple, everyday acts of obedience. Yesterday, during our community session, I was reminded of this lesson once again. I'm still participating in the RDAP (Residential Drug and Alcohol Program), and I had made up my mind to take it easy for the month of June. However, You, God, had other plans.

You allowed a situation to unfold that drew me deeper into the community, and I ended up speaking some important words of truth to a gentleman: "Your image is what you think of yourself. Your reputation is what others think of you. And both of those could be

A New Mission: From Prisoner to Purpose

lies." It was a powerful moment. I could feel You speaking through me, and the message was not just for him, but for many of the men who were listening.

Afterward, several men approached me, thanking me for the words they needed to hear. I knew, Lord, that it wasn't me speaking—it was You, using me as a vessel. What a humbling experience.

Later that day, I had a conversation with Dr. Neller, who oversees the RDAP program. He asked me what I thought about the state of our community, and I told him I believed it was one of the best. Despite the challenging situation we faced, it didn't escalate to violence, and I credit that to the growth we've experienced as a group.

Dr. Neller also mentioned that I will be missed when I leave this place. It's hard to think about leaving behind the bonds I've formed here, but I know my mission is to make an impact in these men's lives. For as long as I am here, Lord, help me continue to do Your work, to be a light in this dark place, and to give all the glory to You.

To God be the glory, always.

June 21, 2011

What an intense few weeks these have been. I mentioned to the chaplain not long ago that I felt a storm brewing, though I didn't know what form it would take or when it would come. Now I understand.

Last Friday, my character was put to the ultimate test. Someone stole the Jewish bread from the chapel, and somehow, my name was the only one that came up

Chapter Twelve

in connection to the theft. It wasn't me, but the accusation stirred up a deep anger inside of me. To be falsely accused is a bitter pill to swallow, and it felt like a knife twisting in my gut. Someone lied about me, and it hurt.

But as the emotions surged, I realized this was my moment to practice discernment, to rise above my anger and examine the hearts and actions of the men around me. So many of them have hidden agendas—wearing masks that hide their true intentions. I know, Lord, that this world is filled with deception, but You have always guided me through the darkness. Now more than ever, I need You to increase in me, Lord. I must decrease daily, surrendering more and more of myself so that I can reflect Your light and Your truth in all circumstances.

In the midst of this turmoil, I received a letter from my family. The enclosed photo brought tears to my eyes: Stephen, my boy, had graduated high school. Despite all of the challenges he faced, he persevered and achieved something truly special. I'm so proud of him. He's accomplished something that so many take for granted, but knowing his struggles, this victory means the world to me.

Some days, it's harder than others to stay focused and push through. The reality of prison life weighs heavily on me. Negativity is a constant companion here, like a thick fog that seeps into every corner. The cussing, the stealing, the lying—it surrounds me. It can be exhausting to simply do right in a world where wrong seems to reign. But I know You're with me, Lord. This is a test—a test of character, and I am being refined like gold in the fire.

A New Mission: From Prisoner to Purpose

Change doesn't happen overnight. It's a slow process, but I know that true transformation begins with You, Jesus. Some days I see evidence of my change, and other days I wonder when it will fully take hold. Lord, keep molding me, keep refining me. I want to be more like You with each passing day.

June 27, 2011

Wow, God! Yesterday I had an experience that I didn't fully understand until today. It started when I was sitting in the rec yard, observing the usual hustle and bustle. There's a young man here that I've noticed for a while. His name is Ben, and he's always loud—his voice filled with negativity, his words laced with profanity. His energy is hard to miss, and not in a good way. But something stirred in me yesterday, and I felt compelled to speak to him.

I called out to him, asking his name. "Ben," he replied, surprised that I even acknowledged him. He asked for my name and why I was interested in talking to him. I told him simply, "I'm a Christian." He seemed to shut down at that, quickly telling me that he wasn't into "that God stuff." But I didn't push. Instead, I asked him if he needed prayer for anything. He hesitated for a moment, then mentioned his children and his family. I promised him I'd pray for them, and we parted ways.

Today, I saw Ben again, but this time, there was a heaviness in his demeanor. He told me that when he called home after our conversation, he learned that a loved one had passed away. He found it strange that I had approached him the day before, asking if he needed prayer, right before he received that devastating news.

Chapter Twelve

I shared with him that sometimes God gives us comfort before we even know we need it—His way of preparing us for the storms ahead.

Thank you, Lord, for speaking to me, for nudging me to reach out to Ben. I didn't know what You had planned, but You did. Thank You for choosing to use me in that moment, to offer a word of prayer and encouragement before the heartache hit. I'm humbled by Your ways, God, and I thank You for the opportunity to be obedient to Your voice. Glory to You, Lord, for using me as Your vessel.

July 5, 2011

"I will never leave you nor forsake you." These words from God have been resonating deeply within me today. I stand firm on His promises, knowing without a doubt that though people, situations, and circumstances may shift and change, God remains steadfast and unchanging. His faithfulness endures through all things.

Last Thursday, June 30, 2011, was a day of answered prayer—the crack law was finally made retroactive. This news was nothing short of a miracle, a long-awaited response to the cries of so many. I have been praying that this change will lead to a reduction in my total sentence and even reduce the five years of federal supervision I'm supposed to serve after my release. With this shift, there's real hope now that I may leave the halfway house earlier than January 2012.

But even as I celebrated this breakthrough, a storm was brewing. A month ago, I sensed it—a test was coming, and I even spoke it out loud, prophesying to myself

A New Mission: From Prisoner to Purpose

that a challenge would soon arise. And sure enough, last Tuesday, my character was under attack. Two men from my housing unit launched their assault, not with fists but with words, laced with accusations and lies. As their voices rose in anger, it became clear to me that this wasn't just a human confrontation—it was a spiritual battle. It was light versus darkness, truth against lies.

Yet in that moment, God filled me with His Spirit, giving me the strength to stand firm and remain calm. It wasn't just about me anymore. The men in the unit, those in the drug program, and the community at large were watching to see how I would handle it. The situation could have easily spiraled into something ugly, but God showed up, guiding me through every second of it. He didn't just protect me—He used me to demonstrate to others how to navigate conflict with grace.

Later, I sat down with Mr. Neller, the man who first encountered me back in the chapel during a service in February 2011. He admitted that I had left a lasting impact on him from that time, which made it all the more painful for him when he witnessed me in a moment of weakness, offending someone. He respected me deeply and was hurt by my actions. That conversation was humbling. It reminded me of the influence I have, even when I'm not fully aware of it. Lord, help me stay focused on You. Help me keep my eyes on Your Word, on Your truth—not on people or the circumstances around me. This is Your church here at Forrest City. Build it as You see fit, Lord.

Most of all, God, You get the glory. You see the hearts of those who have remained faithful, even in this place. You honor commitment and steadfastness. Lord,

Chapter Twelve

continue to work in me and in this community, and let Your will be done.

July 7, 2011

Dear Reverend Barbee,

It was so good to hear from you, and we appreciate the photos of you, your dad, and your brother. You look well, and it's always nice to see those familiar faces. Your baseball stats were impressive, too—it sounds like you've still got your game! It's also a blessing to hear that we can expect you home by this time next year. Praise the Lord! We can hardly wait.

My husband has had a rough month health-wise. He's been quite ill, but we thank God he's finally starting to feel better. Glory to Jesus! At 86, he's been diagnosed with chronic anemia, and the doctors are still unsure of what's causing it. His health takes a real hit when he falls sick, and it's tough watching him go through this. He's lost 24 pounds over the past two years, 14 of them just since March. Please keep him in your prayers, and pray for me, too, as I care for him. It's not easy, but the Lord gives me strength every day.

Mother Washington is still in constant pain, especially in her legs. They're going for a second opinion at KU Medical Center in about 10 days. The doctors here want to do surgery, but we're praying for wisdom and healing. Please keep her and Pastor Washington lifted up in your prayers.

On a happier note, our granddaughter has joined the church! What a blessing that has been for us. One of our friends also became a member, and it seems like God is

A New Mission: From Prisoner to Purpose

growing our congregation bit by bit. Our granddaughter will be baptized this Sunday, on the 10th. She's married to our grandson, who works two Sundays a month, and though he hasn't joined the church yet, we're hopeful that he will. He should be there for her baptism this Sunday.

As for Reverend Miles, he's waiting to hear back from the bus company for a transit position, so he's been absent some Sundays. We continue to pray that he finds stable work soon.

Please write when you have time, Reverend Barbee. We keep you in our prayers every day and look forward to hearing from you again soon.

With love and blessings,
Mother and Pastor Holloman

July 14, 2011

God is working in me, and God is working on me, shaping me to be more Christ-like. I can't always understand why, and sometimes I don't even know how, but today I trust God. That's all I can hold on to, the certainty that He knows better than I ever could.

Yesterday was my 47th birthday. My third birthday behind bars. My last birthday in prison. As I sit here, the weight of that sinks in. Three years, three long years of seeing this day pass within these walls. I treated myself to some nacho cheese dip, a simple thing, but in this place, it felt like a small victory, a flicker of joy in the darkness. But even that joy is fleeting. It's hard to shake the sorrow that hangs over me like a storm cloud.

Chapter Twelve

Thank you, Lord, for keeping me, for loving me through it all. Thank you for allowing me to still hear Your voice, even from here. But hearing is only half the battle. Obedience, Lord—that's my prayer. Help me not only to hear You but to follow You, to obey Your voice in every situation. Every day in this place is a test of faith, a struggle to stay on the path You've laid out for me. But I know, without a shadow of doubt, that You are with me.

July 27, 2011

Sometimes you have to sit yourself down and have a real conversation, a heart-to-heart with your own soul. So, how am I doing? Glad you asked.

I'm feeling angry. Really angry. Cautious, cold-hearted, disappointed, disbelieving, frustrated, lonely, overwhelmed, and sad. I'm surprised by how deeply I feel all these emotions, but I'm also withdrawn—like I've put a wall up between myself and everyone around me. It's a strange mix of being hyper-alert, noticing every tiny detail, but at the same time, I feel disconnected. Social stiffness, they call it. I'm critical. I'm uncaring. It's like I don't even recognize myself sometimes.

Why do I feel like this? Because I'm stuck in this drug program at Forrest City Federal Prison. This place is supposed to show me my flaws—my weaknesses, my bad habits, my unacceptable behavior. It's supposed to provide structure and guidance, and honestly, I know I need it. I need help. I signed up for this program because I wanted a change. I *needed* a change. But now that I'm in it, I feel like everything's crashing down on me.

When I signed that contract, agreeing to follow the

A New Mission: From Prisoner to Purpose

rules and the program, I knew what I was getting into. I knew there would be guidelines to follow, expectations to meet. But what I didn't anticipate was the frustration. Every day feels like driving through a school zone with a speed limit of 20 mph, and watching people zoom by at 60. Do you enforce the law, or do you take down the sign? What's the point of having rules if no one is going to follow them?

That's where all this anger and disappointment are coming from. I've placed expectations on myself, and without realizing it, I've transferred those expectations to others. I call it a false expectation. It's like I'm judging the men around me, holding them to a standard that I can barely meet myself. I try not to be prejudiced, but their actions—the stealing, the lying, the negativity—they make me recoil. I distance myself from them, thinking that by doing so, I'm somehow staying clean, staying right.

But am I? Can I honestly say I'm doing right just because I'm not *doing* wrong? The truth is, I've become numb to the wrong around me. I'm callous. I see it, I feel it, and yet, I'm indifferent to it. It's like I'm wearing blinders, pretending that all this negativity isn't affecting me. But it is. It's sinking in, deep. It's shaping how I look at the world and the people in it.

Is that normal? Is that right? My belief system tells me no. But can that system change? Yes. Does it *need* to change? Absolutely. I need to learn to be more understanding, more patient with those around me. But how? How do I deal with all this wrong, this constant cloud of negativity that looms over everything in this place? I know I can't control anyone else—not their actions, not

Chapter Twelve

their behavior. But I can control myself.

Yet, even knowing that, it's so hard. I can't even find a quiet place to study, to concentrate, to clear my mind. Everywhere I turn, there's something pulling me down—people smoking, people working out like it's their religion, people getting tattoos, kitchen workers stealing food and making deals under the table. It's everywhere, this sense of lawlessness, and it's suffocating.

I've distanced myself from it, but in doing so, I've distanced myself from almost everyone. The old saying goes, "The company you keep reveals who you are." I can't keep that company anymore, but now I feel alone. My convictions are too strong to ignore, but are my expectations too high? Is real change even possible in a place like this?

How will I know when I'm changing? Will it feel like a sudden breakthrough, or will it creep up on me slowly, over time? Only time will tell, I guess. But one thing I know for sure—I'm not going to let this place define me. I'm not going to let the wrong around me become the wrong within me. I'm holding on, Lord. I'm holding on to the hope that change *is* possible, and that You're not done with me yet.

On the night of July 31, 2011, a moment of divine clarity came to me while I was incarcerated in Forrest City, Arkansas. I awoke from a vivid dream around 3:30 a.m., where I saw a young man from my unit needing to defend himself for his ongoing wrongdoings and justify why he shouldn't be removed from the drug program. The dream was strikingly detailed, leaving me with a strong sense of purpose that it wasn't just a random vi-

A New Mission: From Prisoner to Purpose

sion but a message from God. I felt compelled to find the young man and share the dream with him.

Later that day, around 12:15 pm, I finally encountered the young man and began recounting the dream. As I spoke, the man opened up about his personal life. He revealed the deep burdens he was carrying—family struggles, broken relationships, and the overwhelming weight of the life he had lived before prison. I felt a heavy presence of God in that moment and warned the young man that if he was still involved in wrongdoing, he needed to stop because God had sent the dream as a warning.

As the man talked about his fears and the dangers awaiting him back in his city, I could see the fear in his eyes—fear of life and death situations that were all too real. In response, I offered him the comfort of prayer, asking God to remove his fear and the weight of his burdens. We prayed together, and in the young man's tear-filled eyes, I witnessed the power of God's presence, reassuring him that he was not alone. I made myself available as a listening ear, someone the man could talk to whenever he needed support.

On that same day, while I was brushing my teeth, the voice of God whispered to me that Garrison, another man in the unit, needed prayer. Garrison had been acting irritable for a while and had lost his appetite, which concerned me. That afternoon, I found Garrison in the TV room and asked to speak with him. Together, we prayed for healing, asking God to restore Garrison's appetite and give him comfort. Remarkably, later that day, Garrison shared that he had rested for over four hours, feeling a deep sense of peace. Leo felt God's Spirit moving in

Chapter Twelve

powerful ways, not just within himself, but in the lives of those around him.

Fast forward to August 12, 2011, and the dream about the young man came true. The man was called into the office to defend himself to the staff for the wrongs he had continued to commit, just as I had seen in my dream. The experience reinforced for me that God was using me as an instrument to share wisdom and insight through the gift of words of knowledge. With this realization, Leo knew that God had restored his spiritual gifts, and they were growing stronger day by day.

His commitment to "dying to himself daily" and following Jesus was now deeper than ever. I recognized that each day was an opportunity to pick up my cross, surrender my own will, and allow God's purpose to work through me for the good of others. This period in my life became a testament to God's faithfulness, as I learned to fully embrace the gifts given to me for God's glory, trusting that every encounter was part of a larger divine plan.

August 23, 2011: A Year at Forrest City

The oppressive heat of an Arkansas summer clung to the air as I marked a full year of my life behind the heavy iron gates of Forrest City federal prison. As I reflected on the past 12 months, it felt like a surreal journey, a strange and difficult pilgrimage through a wilderness of steel and concrete. The days had been long, but they hadn't passed without meaning. In fact, each day had been a lesson—an opportunity for God to reveal more of Himself and teach me who I was becoming in Christ.

A New Mission: From Prisoner to Purpose

It was as if I had been enrolled in a divine classroom, with the Lord as my Teacher, using the circumstances of prison life to refine me. The words of the Apostle Paul echoed in my mind: *"Forgetting those things which are behind, and pressing on toward the mark."* I know this truth well now. There was no room for regret or dwelling on past mistakes; the only direction was forward, toward the high calling of Christ. Yet, that didn't mean it was easy.

I had seen and experienced relationships in this place that were built on conditions, alliances formed out of survival rather than love. It hurt, but I knew that in each of these encounters, my goal was to respond in a Christ-like way, no matter the cost. I made a conscious decision to set aside pride, bitterness, or self-pity.

God didn't let up on testing me, and sometimes the tests came without warning. I often wouldn't recognize them until after the storm had passed, when I could look back and see what God had been doing. The loneliness, too, was a test. It felt like isolation, but I had come to understand that it was separation for preparation—God was molding me for something greater. The evil and darkness that surrounded me in prison made the need for constant prayer all the more urgent. Prayer was my lifeline. I had a direct connection to God in this desolate place. The Word of God became my shield, and Leo had to "be prayed up and Word up," ready for the spiritual battles that surrounded him.

I knew that doubt, disbelief, and disobedience had no place in his life. My faith needed to be unwavering. I also wrestled with receiving blessings, learning that sometimes God's work came through others, and I had

Chapter Twelve

to humble myself to accept help. All of these tests were shaping my character, transforming me into the person God intended for me to be. I prayed that my life would reflect God's glory, that even in this dark place, I could be a beacon of light. The prayer ended with the quiet certainty of surrender: *"Amen."*

August 31, 2011: A Letter from the Outside

The days blurred together at Forrest City, but I could still feel the pull of life outside the walls, especially when letters from loved ones reached me. The familiar handwriting on the envelope instantly reminded me of home. It was a letter from Pastor Holloman and Mother Washington, those dear saints who had always been spiritual pillars in my life. I could almost hear their voices as I unfolded the pages.

"Dear Reverend Barbee, my goodness, where has this year gone?"

I smiled. Time was a funny thing in prison—slow and monotonous, yet somehow a year had passed in what seemed like the blink of an eye. I read on, feeling the warmth and care in every word. Pastor Holloman had recovered from his illness and was back to full strength, even gaining weight again. My heart swelled with gratitude for answered prayers. Mother Washington was traveling for revival in Flint, Michigan, but would soon undergo back surgery. I immediately committed to lifting her in prayer, knowing the Lord's hand was already at work in her healing. The mention of Sister Dia, whose cancer had returned, made me pause. Another weight to carry, another name to bring before God in prayer.

A New Mission: From Prisoner to Purpose

It was bittersweet hearing about the children's department at the church, a ministry close to my heart. The department was thriving, putting on monthly programs under the diligent work of Sister Dahlia and Brother Jason. My heart felt a pang of longing—I missed the vibrant energy of working with the youth, seeing their growth in faith. Yet, I also knew that God was using me here in prison, and my prayers for the children back home were still powerful.

The letter closed with the same words of encouragement that had kept me going over the past year: *"We continue to pray that the Lord will use you daily for His glory."* I folded the letter and held it in my hands, whispering a prayer for everyone mentioned. Even behind these walls, I was still connected to the body of Christ, still part of something larger, still held in the grace of God's hands.

September 5, 2011: My Last Labor Day in Prison

As I sit here in this small, confined space, looking out the window at a world that's beyond my reach, I can't help but reflect on what this day signifies. It's my last Labor Day in prison, and for that, I praise the Lord. His word tells me to *"give thanks in all circumstances, for this is God's will for you in Christ Jesus."* I cling to that truth today. Just a few months ago, I found myself saying out loud, "I hate prison, but I will not waste prison." And here I am, still holding fast to that commitment.

Looking out at the sky beyond the prison walls, I see the hope of a new start, a fresh beginning, a renewal. Every day is a gift of renewal, and I choose to embrace it. But as I walk through these halls and hear the con-

Chapter Twelve

stant hum of conversations—*ear hustling,* they call it—it saddens me. So many of the men around me glorify the wrong things: money, drugs, guns, and women. It's not that I wish any of them to return to this place, but their conversations tell me they might. They haven't yet learned what I've come to realize.

I think back to all the things I took for granted—freedom, family, choices. Here, I live with five pairs of shoes, government-issued khakis, underwear, and socks. It's not much, but I've come to understand that regardless of how I got here, the Bureau of Prisons sees us all the same—criminals who broke the law. But praise God, because He sees differently. Today, I know who I am and *whose* I am. I am crucified with Christ, but I am also raised with Christ. I know my position in Him, and I strive daily to bring my condition in line with that truth.

I don't know what awaits me after I'm released, but I know this: God didn't bring me through this to keep me silent. I'm meant to carry the message. My life has been shaped by trials, and these tests are developing me into the man God created me to be. Every moment in this place is meant to refine me, and for that, I give thanks.

September 11, 2011: A Prayer for the Future

Thank you, Lord, for restoring me. The day of my release is drawing near, and with each passing moment, I know I need to walk by faith more than ever. My faith walk determines my destiny. Yesterday, while I was in the shower, the Holy Spirit prompted me to pray for my future wife. I don't know who she is, but God, You do. I ask You to prepare her heart to receive me, to love me, encourage me, and support me. She must be a godly

A New Mission: From Prisoner to Purpose

woman, rooted in You, knowing her identity in Christ.

Today, as I woke up and went to the recreation yard, I found a place on the bleachers where I could worship You in peace. I opened Your word and read through Psalm 119, praying and meditating on Your promises. But even there, as I was worshiping, the darkness of this place made itself known. A group of men, so-called gang members, gathered nearby, plotting and planning evil. My heart grieves for them. Lord, let Your light shine in their hearts. Convict them of their wrongdoing and save them, just as You have saved me.

As I sit here, I also thank You for what lies ahead. I trust You, Lord, to provide for me—a job, a home, a community of believers. Your word promises that You have begun a good work in me, and I trust that You will complete it. Amen.

September 12, 2011: Meeting with God in the Yard

Thank you, Lord, for Your word and for the Holy Spirit who guides me daily. Yesterday, I woke up with a word from You: "Go to the recreation yard, and I will meet you there." It was Sunday, a day I usually dedicate to going to church, but I felt strongly that I needed to obey the voice of the Holy Spirit. So I went to the yard, found a spot on the bleachers, and opened my Bible.

As I read Psalm 120, especially verse two, it was as if You were speaking directly to me, reminding me that Your promises are always yes and amen. As I worship You in spirit and truth, I could feel the presence of evil around me. Another inmate, under the influence of the

Chapter Twelve

enemy, pointed at me and lied about me. But instead of reacting, as the old me would have, I continued to pray and thank You. The new me is learning to let go, to give it all to You. I no longer feel the need to defend myself. I trust You, Lord, to be my defense. Amen.

October 8, 2011: Nearing the End of This Journey

Bless the Lord, oh my soul. As my release date draws near, I feel the weight of this transition. I need to stay focused and remain steadfast in prayer and Your word. You have freed me, Lord—not just from these walls, but from the chains that held me captive in my mind and spirit. Now, I surrender completely to Your plan and purpose for my life.

Reveal to me, God, Your thoughts towards me as I continue to seek You. The trials I've faced, the lessons You've taught me—they're all part of the bigger picture. I need to die to myself daily, and as You reveal more of Yourself to me, I know I am held accountable to live in obedience to Your word.

Yesterday, I had the chance to talk with my son, Steven. He sounded good, and we had a great conversation about his job and, of course, the twins. His excitement about the girls brought a smile to my face. I also told him about the possibility of being released next month. I could hear the hope in his voice, but I reminded him, and myself, that it's all in God's hands. Not my will, but Yours be done, Lord. Amen.

October 12, 2011: Preparing for the Future

As I hit the track, my shoes crunching against the

A New Mission: From Prisoner to Purpose

gravel and the cool early morning air filling my lungs, I dropped down for another set of push-ups. Each rep felt purposeful, like a prayer rising up with each press. And then, in the quiet space between breaths, the Lord spoke. "Save yourself for your wife to be," He said. I stopped for a moment, absorbing His words. My heart filled with gratitude as I realized He was preparing me, even now, for something beautiful in the future. *"Lord, I thank You,"* I whispered, knowing He was shaping me to become the godly man needed to lead a marriage.

As I walked the track, the conversations of the men around me faded into the background. They often talked about overcoming battles, but it wasn't always the kind of victory I sought. Their minds were still wrapped up in the things of the world—drugs, money, and women. But I had a different victory in mind. The Lord was preparing me for something far deeper, and all I needed to do was be obedient when the time came. *"Thank you in advance for Mrs. Barbee, Lord,"* I prayed, a smile creeping across my face as I imagined the future.

October 15, 2011: Loss and Reflection

Yesterday, I found out that Uncle Bob passed away, and just five weeks after that, Aunt Star followed him. My heart is heavy, even as I sit in this prison cell. Just a few weeks ago, they were on my mind and heart. I had told myself that when I got out, the first place I needed to visit was Neosho, to see them. Life is so fragile, and death has a way of reminding you how quickly things change. I didn't get to say goodbye, but I know they're with the Lord now.

My prison term is winding down, and with that

comes a sharpened sense of focus. The enemy is angry, and I can feel the distractions circling like vultures, waiting for a moment of weakness. But I won't give in. I thank God for His protection, for keeping me anchored in His word. I'm also grateful for my work in the chapel. Serving there has given me purpose, a place to lead and encourage others. *"Thank you, Lord, for placing me in the chapel to serve. Keep me strong and focused as I finish this journey."*

October 23, 2011: Early Morning Prayer

It's 4:00 am, but the Lord woke me up at 3:00. I knew deep down that He wanted me to spend time with Him this morning. As I lay there, I felt the pull to get up, to listen, to pray. So here I am, sitting in the stillness, waiting to hear what He has to say. *"Speak, Lord, Your servant is listening."*

Earlier this week, while I was in prayer and reading the Word, the Lord directed me to go and pray with Kendall. I didn't hesitate. I found him, and we prayed together. At first, we thought it was about a decision he had to make when signing out of the program. But two days later, it became clear. A co-defendant who had testified against Kendall showed up on the compound—the same man who contributed to Kendall's lengthy sentence. The real decision was about forgiveness. And when we talked, Kendall made a choice: he was willing to forgive.

Later that day, another man in my housing unit approached me. He asked if I could pray for his mother, who was in the hospital with kidney failure. We prayed together, and last night, with tears in his eyes, he told me her kidneys had started functioning again. God had heard our prayers, and I couldn't help but praise Him for His faithfulness. *"The prayers of the righteous prevail, Lord. Amen."*

October 27, 2011: God's Spirit Moving

Wow. God, You are awesome. What a week it's been. Last Sunday, October 23, the Lord laid it on my heart to ask the chaplain if we could hold a service on Tuesday. I wasn't sure what he would say, but I asked in faith. He thought about it and then said, "Yes!" I could hardly believe it. I immediately asked five other brothers to join me in speaking, and we invited the praise team to lead worship.

When Tuesday came, the Spirit of God filled that place. Brother Samuel spoke about Christ coming in the flesh, Brother Felipe talked about the crucifixion, J.R. covered the pride of man, Brother Al broke down humility, and I closed out the service with a testimony of God's work in our lives. The power of God was undeniable. It felt like heaven had touched down in the chapel. Every man who spoke carried the weight of God's message on their lips, and we left that service changed.

Later, Aunt Judy had been heavy on my heart, so I called her. She picked up after two rings, and her voice was a balm to my soul. *"Nephew,"* she said, just like she always does, and we laughed as we caught up. She told me they had been talking about me just the day before—how God works in mysterious ways.

But even in the midst of this joy, I feel a pressing call from God. He has been building a platform for me, not just in this place, but for when I leave. The challeng-

Chapter Twelve

es He has laid on my heart aren't small, but I trust that He will guide me when the time comes to speak. *"Lord, show me when to share, what to share, and how to share it. Let Your will be done. Amen, Amen!"*

October 28, 2011

To hear the voice of God is one thing, but to obey it—that's where the true test lies. Just the other day, I kept hearing the voice of Laura, clear as day, telling me to put a picture in my pocket. He told me I would see T and Adam. Sure enough, after I came out of chow, there they were. That moment made me realize God is waiting for people who will obey, not just hear. It filled me with joy knowing I heard His voice and acted on it. Lately, He's been waking me earlier and earlier. I've been using that time in prayer and reading the Word. I can't fully see what's ahead, but I trust the Lord because He's in control. God, Your will be done in my life.

November 1, 2011

Yesterday, I officially began phase three of the residential drug and alcohol program here at Forrest City. This final phase is where everything comes together, and I know God has me here for a reason. Influence. I know He didn't call me to be normal, but to be different in His kingdom—abnormal in the best way, because different is what brings Him glory. Just like a good lead-off hitter, starting a rally, God has placed me in this role as a co-facilitator this week and next week, to set the tone. I can see it clearly now. With new people coming in and others leaving, my prayer is simple: all of You, Lord, and none of me. The Spirit of God rests in my heart, speaks to me clearly, and I know I'm meant to help these men see Jesus and feel His presence. Let healing, deliverance, and salvation come to this drug program—that's my prayer.

November 11, 2011

Lord, I thank You for being my Lord and Savior. I'm grateful for the things You've revealed to me and even for the things You've kept hidden. The question echoing in my mind: Do you trust Me? With just 68 days left on my sentence, I've been experiencing God in ways I never imagined. He's protected me, provided for me, guided me, and yes, He's broken me too. But He's also filled me with His Holy Spirit.

Just last week, my monthly pay came in. I was shocked—but I shouldn't have been. God doesn't share His glory; He's always in control. I remember when my pay was just $3 or $7 a month. But this time, it was $118. God is able to do far more than we can ask or imagine. And it's not just the money—He's been providing in ways I didn't expect. Even though I only make a small amount, I've never missed a quarterly payment on my fine, because God has always provided. These past two weeks as co-facilitator and facilitator have been meaningful because I know lasting change, real change, only comes through Christ.

There's so much wrong in the world around me, but God's Spirit keeps reminding me: be a sermon. Let them see Jesus in you. I believe that through prayer, many of these men will change. I spent time with Brother Mike in the library this week, and it was clear that God had a different purpose for me being there. We had great fellowship in the Lord.

Chapter Twelve

But my heart is heavy for Jim, a young man in bondage to pornography. Day in and day out, he feeds his mind with it. I told him God loves him, and I'm praying for him daily because I've been there too. God delivered me, and He can deliver Jim. An older gentleman also self-surrendered this week, and I saw the fear in his eyes. I recognized it because I've been there. Lord, let me serve him, bring him peace.

November 25, 2011

As one door closes, God opens another. I'm nearing the end of my time here, and yesterday I had my last Thanksgiving meal in prison. Chaplain Ford preached about being thankful, no matter where you are, and I truly am. I see life from a whole new perspective. So many of these men are caught up in their image, their reputation, worried about what the next man thinks or says. But I thank God today that He's delivered me from people's opinions. For so long, I gave people power over me, and it kept me in bondage. Now, all I care about is what God thinks of me and what He says I am.

Yesterday, I called Dad and Miss Helen, not knowing they were in St. Louis visiting Stephen, Sherell, Renee, and Ryeanna—seeing my grandchildren. It made my day, just knowing they were all together. I'm so close to the end now. I need to stay focused, keep my ears and eyes open to God's voice, and remain obedient. Lord, use me as a vessel to bring You glory.

November 25, 2011

It was a typical Sunday night when Brother Johnson came over to the chapel. He wanted to watch a movie, but before we could settle in, he asked me to pray for him. As soon as he made the request, I felt the Lord's voice stirring within me. Without hesitation, I stood up, placed my hand on his shoulder, and said, "Let's pray." I could feel the Spirit moving through me as I began to pray for his family, asking God to provide a supernatural blessing.

Today, Johnson approached me again, his face lit up with excitement. "Brother," he said, "My wife just received a settlement check—$4,000! We were only expecting $1,000!" He was amazed, but I wasn't. I knew it was God's hand at work, His supernatural provision coming through once again. Hearing Johnson's testimony filled me with a renewed sense of God's power and grace.

November 27, 2011

God's timing is perfect. It was early this morning, around 4:30 a.m., when I was abruptly awakened by the Lord's voice, clear as day: "Get up." I rolled over and glanced at the clock. It was still dark outside, but I knew better than to ignore that call. I got up and began my devotional, seeking His presence in the quiet of the morning.

As I read through my Bible, two scriptures stood out to me: Luke 12:38 and 1 Thessalonians 5:6. Both verses carried the same word—watch. In one, a servant is told to watch faithfully, and in the other, believers are called to watch soberly. I pondered the meaning of this, letting the word settle in my spirit, when suddenly I heard the sound of keys jingling.

Chapter Twelve

I looked up and saw a CO walking toward me. "Inmate Barbee?" he asked. I nodded. "You need to get dressed. You're needed at the suicide watch station."

That's when it clicked—the "watch" in those scriptures wasn't just spiritual. It was literal. God had spoken to me about being vigilant, about being a watchman, and now I was being called to watch over a young man on suicide watch. It was no coincidence. When God speaks, He moves, and things happen.

This week, God has been speaking to me about marriage, of all things. It's been on my mind, and on three separate occasions, He's told me to wait. Each time, He impressed upon me that my future wife will come to me in a way that's unusual, uncommon. Just like a woman in labor, where each contraction brings her closer to giving birth, I feel like I'm nearing a new chapter in my life. With my prison term coming to an end, life is about to be birthed in a new way. Life is here, and I'm ready.

December 10, 2011

Yesterday, I felt an overwhelming urge to call my son, Stephen. When I did, I wasn't prepared for the news he gave me. My oldest nephew, Skyler, had taken his own life. That wasn't the news I expected, and it hit hard. I called my brother, and he told me more—Skyler had shot a police officer and then turned the gun on himself. It still hasn't fully sunk in. Skyler was raised by my parents, and even though he had a rough patch at times, he was always a good kid. It's heartbreaking. This is a time of deep prayer for me.

Just recently, Mother Holloman sent me a letter,

A New Mission: From Prisoner to Purpose

telling me her grandson also committed suicide last month. It's clear to me now—the enemy knows his time is short, and he's working overtime to take as many lives as he can. As I sit here in prison, I see the broken hearts and troubled minds of men all around me. It's true—prison doesn't change men. Only Christ can change a man's heart.

I'm surrounded by anger, bitterness, guilt, shame, and the weight of a victim mentality. God, keep me safe in this place. Those who refuse to accept their circumstances, who blame everyone else for their problems, remain stuck in that victim mindset. God, I pray You free my mind and spirit through the blood of Christ and Your Word. I see firsthand how negative peer pressure can grip a man and lead him to do terrible things. Every day, I witness men here fall into patterns of behavior that are nothing but destructive.

It's been a wake-up call for me—God has shown me where I was and where I was headed. I see men who leave here, only to return not long after. Lord, I'm thankful for these 44 months You've given me to sit down, be disciplined, and be taught by You. I know it's because You love me. I don't know what's next, but I'm excited—excited about what You've already done in my life and what You're about to do. On January 18, I'll be leaving here, and I'm stepping out in faith with expectation. I believe You're going to open doors for me—for employment, for a place to stay, for a wife, and for the fulfillment of my calling.

December 18, 2011

Last night, as I lay in my bunk, I prayed, "Lord,

Chapter Twelve

when You wake me up, I'll spend that time with You." Be careful what you ask for! Sure enough, the Lord woke me up at 2:30 a.m. So here I am, in the back room, reading my Word, praying, and meditating on God. God, You are so good. He's been revealing to me that my time in prison wasn't a death sentence—it's been a pathway to everlasting life.

I know there are people who will keep their distance from me because of my time in prison, but God has shown me that He'll bring new people into my life, people who are drawn to Him because of my experiences. Today, I'm 30 days from the door. Even as I walk through this final stretch, I'm being tested. Just the other day, another inmate—Warren L.—called me out, mocking me, calling me weak, using slurs, and calling me a Christian. But I didn't say a word. His words weren't really about me; they were about Christ living in me.

I'm still processing the pain of losing Skyler. It hurts deeply, but I have to trust God and draw my strength from Him. Mr. Haskins said something on Friday that stuck with me: "The bigger the test, the bigger the impact you'll make in life." The enemy's distractions are all around me, even in the small things happening at the chapel. But I thank God for bringing Brother Tamar Brown into the unit. Tamar loves the Lord as much as I do, and we've connected over our shared faith. Just like the scripture says, "As iron sharpens iron, so one person sharpens another." I pray the Lord will allow Tamar to sharpen me as I sharpen him.

God, I thank You for my dear brother Tamar. I pray for his protection, that You'll provide for him in every way. Thank You, Lord, for placing people in my life who

A New Mission: From Prisoner to Purpose

love You and push me closer to You.

Chapter Twelve

Chapter THIRTEEN

MY LIGHT SHINING IN PRISON

I sat quietly, in the housing of the unit around me just background noise, lost in the rhythm of daily life in prison. The envelope sat in my lap, simple but heavy with anticipation. The question I'd asked was straightforward: "How have I impacted your life?" But the answers—well, I didn't know what to expect. Slowly, I opened the first letter, and as my eyes began to scan the words, my heart stirred.

The first man wrote about how he'd watched me. Not just once or twice, but *watched*. He'd seen me pray, not just with words but with my whole being. He spoke of moments in the chapel, on the rec yard, in the day-to-day grind, where he could feel the Spirit flow through me. I wasn't just talking about God; I was walking it. He said he saw something he didn't think was possible—a man truly living for the Lord in a place designed to strip

Chapter Thirteen

us of our humanity, of our hope.

I paused for a moment, absorbing his words. It's not easy to live out faith here, where anger, despair, and hatred cling to every corner. But he saw it. He saw the love of God extend across racial lines, across barriers that would normally keep men like us apart. And he was proud to call me his brother. He said he'd see me in heaven one day. I closed my eyes, feeling the weight of those words, the connection that transcends this place.

I moved to the second letter. This man remembered the day we met, how he immediately recognized something different in me. He saw how I obeyed Jesus no matter the cost, even if it meant standing alone. There were days when I felt that loneliness, days when I wondered if anyone even noticed, if what I was doing mattered. But he noticed. He called it a testimony, one that reminded him to keep Jesus at the center, no matter what the world throws our way. He wrote that I was proof—proof that the Lord always has one faithful servant left, no matter how dark the times.

The third letter struck me like a thunderclap. This man didn't just thank me; he thanked God for the work He was doing through us. *Us.* It wasn't just about me. God was moving in all of us. He said meeting me was a blessing, a privilege to witness someone walking upright, in integrity, no matter the cost. I swallowed hard. I knew my time here was drawing to a close, but his words felt prophetic. He said my work was almost complete here, and God had more for me—something bigger, something waiting beyond these walls. "Don't lose focus," he wrote. Those words were a warning and a promise, all in one.

The fourth letter was filled with praise for God and His handiwork, reminding me that every step we take is under His watchful eye. This man saw me as an example, a man standing for truth over feelings. That hit me deep. It's easy to let emotions guide us, especially in a place where anger simmers just beneath the surface. But he saw me standing firm, grounded in something more. He prayed for my humility, for my eyes to stay open as I stepped into the next chapter of my life. The devil prowls, especially when we're on the verge of something new. His words reminded me to stay vigilant, to trust that God's positioning is never by accident.

As I read the fifth letter, a different tone emerged. This man was honest—brutally so. He spoke of the good and the bad, how knowing me had forced him to confront his own choices. He appreciated my honesty, my willingness to call him out when he needed it. He admitted that seeing me and what I had been through, the choices I'd made—was a wake-up call. "One bad choice," he wrote, "and I could be back here." It was a sobering reminder that freedom, both in the physical and spiritual, is fragile. His words inspired me as much as he claimed I inspired him. We were in this fight together, fighting for our souls, for our futures, for a life beyond these fences.

The last letter was like a balm to my soul. This man didn't just see me as a fellow inmate; he saw me as an angel, a vessel sent by God to open his eyes. He spoke of being blessed, of seeing something in me that made him believe in his own ability to change. And then he said something that hit me in the gut: "If you ever have a doubt that your life hasn't fully turned around, this letter is your proof." My breath caught. How many times had I questioned if I was really on the right path? How many

Chapter Thirteen

times had I wondered if God was truly using me? His letter was an answer—a divine reminder that none of this was in vain.

I sat back, the weight of their words were pressing down on me, but in the best way. These men—these brothers—had witnessed my journey. They had seen me stumble, rise, and stand firm. And in that process, they found something for themselves: hope, faith, a reason to believe that even here, in this prison, God was at work.

As I folded the last letter, I knew one thing for sure: this wasn't about me. It never had been. God had woven our lives together for a purpose, His purpose. And even in the darkest, most unexpected places, His light shines. Through me, through them, through all of us.

January 1, 2012

It's a new year, and I can finally say it: No more. No more guest bags. No more holiday meals. Yesterday, I ate my last one, and I still can't believe they served us steak. It was surreal knowing that would be my final holiday meal behind these walls. I finished my last work detail, too. Now, all that's left are two more Sunday services and seven community meetings before I graduate from the residential drug and alcohol program. It's hard to believe this chapter is almost over, but I'm ready. "I thank You, Lord, for everything You've brought me through."

The details I shared capture a pivotal time of transition and anticipation for what lies ahead, before my graduation.

January 12, 2012

Last Thursday, I was working out when I heard this clear message: "Being overconfident is the first setback." It stuck with me. I know the enemy will come at me through many doors, but the key is guarding my flesh. As I prepare to leave this place, I'm filled with excitement and anticipation, not fear. I'm looking forward to what God has planned for me on the outside—my employment, my family, and new relationships. I know that wherever He takes me next, it's all for His glory.

By January 12, 2012, my focus shifted to preparing for life after prison. I wisely acknowledged the dangers of overconfidence and recognized how easily setbacks could come, especially through the vulnerabilities of the flesh.

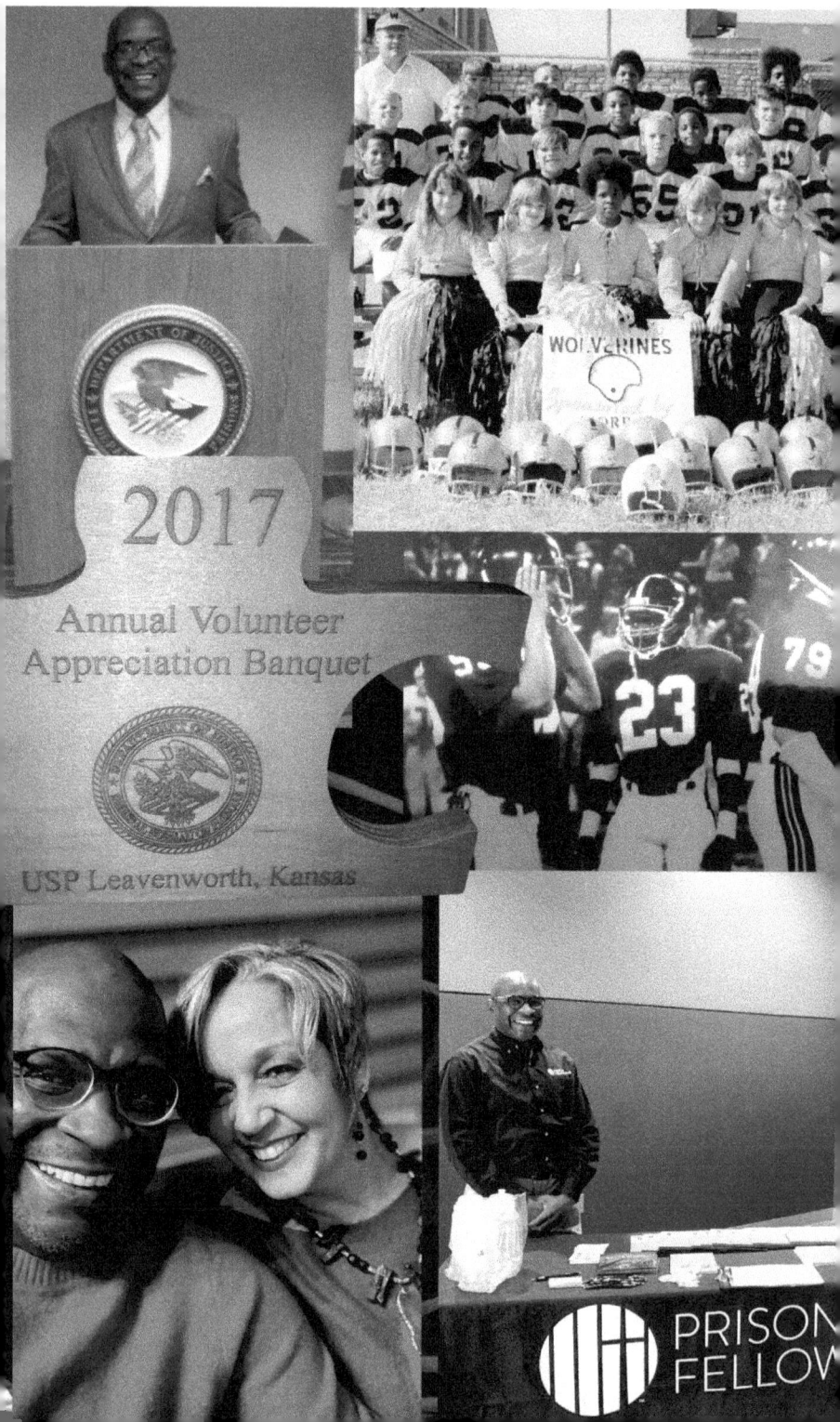

Chapter FOURTEEN

THE REBUILDING: SECOND CHANCE & THE CHALLENGE OF REENTRY

January 17, 2012

I received a letter today from Mother and Pastor Holloman. They're so excited that I'm getting closer to home. Mother shared that my dad is happy to have me nearer. It warmed my heart to know they've been praying for me. They asked me to pray with them for the New Beginning Church—they're fasting and praying for God's wisdom and provision to build their new property, debt-free. I love their faith.

Mother Washington is recovering from surgery, and Pastor Holloman is back at the Senate, serving as chaplain for his 31st year. They even mentioned watching a

Chapter Fourteen

Kansas game, which made me smile. That's something we always did together, watch sports.

They asked if I'd come visit when I get to leave the halfway house. I'm looking forward to the day I can walk through those church doors and hug them both. They've been such a pillar of faith in my life. For now, I'll keep pressing forward, trusting that God has great things in store. Each day brings me closer to the life He's prepared for me.

The letter from Mother and Pastor Holloman on January 17, 2012, is heartwarming. Their excitement about my return to Kansas City made freedom palpable. They share updates on family, church, and health, underscoring their deep connection to me. Their prayerful request for guidance in building a debt-free church and their encouragement for my ministry once I am released show a supportive community eager to welcome me back with open arms. The personal touches—like references to watching Kansas games and Pastor Holloman's Senate chaplaincy—illustrate the care they have for me, praying for my success and joyfully awaiting my return. It's clear that I will be stepping into a new chapter of life, filled with hope, faith, and the unwavering support of loved ones.

Leaving prison after 44 months was a mixture of anticipation, anxiety, and uncertainty. The journey began with receiving furlough papers from Federal Correction Institution Forrest City, Arkansas, marking my transition from incarceration to a kind of temporary freedom. I wasn't fully free yet, but there was hope in the unknown. Boarding the bus to Little Rock, my mind raced with thoughts of how my reentry into society would unfold.

The Rebuilding: Second Chance & the Challenge of ReEntry

Each town we passed, each moment staring out the window, felt surreal.

The most poignant moment came when the bus passed through Springfield, Missouri. I imagined my beloved Aunt Janet Sue parked in her car nearby, but I couldn't even get off the bus to hug her. The feeling of separation was bittersweet—freedom so close, yet out of reach.

Stopping in Clinton, Missouri, I was finally able to eat a simple sandwich with potato chips—a small but significant taste of freedom. Yet, I couldn't shake the feeling that I wasn't truly free. My 12-hour furlough was a ticking clock; I had to report to the halfway house at 1514 Campbell Street in Kansas City, Missouri, by 8:05 PM. If I arrived even five minutes late, it would mean facing an escape charge, with the U.S. Marshals hot on my trail.

When the bus pulled into the Kansas City Greyhound station, the first sight of my family—my father, Mrs. Helen, and my sister Vicky—flooded me with emotion. We embraced, but even in that moment, reality hit when my dad asked, "Where's your luggage?" I looked him in the eye and replied, "Dad, this is all I have," showing him my release papers, toiletries, and the few personal items I owned. It felt like such a contrast to what I had imagined freedom to be, I didn't have it all, but a few items to my name.

Time was still against me, and I couldn't afford to delay. I had to get to the halfway house before the curfew. My father wanted to take me to get something to eat, but I had to refuse, explaining that if I was late—

Chapter Fourteen

even by minutes—I could end up back in prison.

Arriving at the halfway house, I was met with the harsh reminder that I was still under the system's control. The pat-down, strip search, and drug test reinforced the notion that my freedom was conditional. I was processed and shown to my dormitory, a room shared with 10 or 12 other federal inmates. Lying in that bunk, I couldn't help but wonder what the future held for me. My first night in Kansas City was filled with uncertainty and a lingering sense of being trapped between two worlds—freedom and incarceration.

The following weeks were filled with more bureaucratic hurdles and reminders of my status as an ex-felon. I needed to get a job, but how could I without proper identification? I only had my Social Security card from prison. My counselor at the halfway house mocked my efforts to reenter society, telling me that I couldn't even start the process without a state ID or birth certificate. It felt like an insurmountable challenge.

Determined, I walked from 1514 Campbell to 2400 Troost Avenue to get my birth certificate. When I finally returned to the halfway house with the document, the counselor smirked and asked, "Where's your state ID?" It felt like a never-ending game. The next day, I walked to the DMV, anxious about the limited time I had on my three-hour pass. When I handed the woman behind the counter my prison ID, I felt a deep sense of shame. But to my surprise, she smiled and said, "Welcome home." Those words felt like a small victory. With my birth certificate, social security card, and state ID in hand, I finally felt a step closer to rebuilding my life.

Yet, the barriers of being a felon loomed largely over my efforts to start a new life. Searching for jobs, I quickly realized how difficult it would be. At the Goodwill center, I spent days on the computer applying for positions, but the system felt stacked against me. When I asked for bus passes to continue my job search, the counselor told me I didn't qualify because I was a federal release, not from the state. It was disheartening to hear that I wasn't eligible for help. Still, before I left that day, the counselor handed me an application for the City Union Mission—another small step in a long journey toward true freedom.

The path of reentry wasn't just about getting a job or finding a place to live. It was about navigating a world that still viewed me as an inmate, as a felon, as someone less than free. But with each step, no matter how small, I began to reclaim my life, determined to prove that my second chance was more than just a brief furlough—it was the start of a new chapter.

In the weeks following my release from prison and adjustment to life in the halfway house in Kansas City, Missouri, I began to take in my surroundings with fresh eyes. Every moment felt significant—each encounter, each new experience shaping my reentry into society. It had been three weeks since I left the walls of federal prison behind, and while I was no longer incarcerated, I was still navigating a system with rules and restrictions that reminded me of my past.

February 13, 2012

Marked a moment of reflection. I had seen my family—my father, Mrs. Helen, my sister Vicki, my son

Chapter Fourteen

Steven, John Brent, and even Sadie and J2. Each reunion was a reminder of God's grace of the people He had placed in my life to support and guide me. The rules at the halfway house felt restrictive at times, but after enduring 44 months in a federal prison, these rules seemed minor. In fact, they were helping me maintain focus, teaching me discipline, and encouraging me to walk by faith. God's presence was so evident to me in those moments; I knew He had brought me to Kansas City for a reason and a season, and I had to trust His will over my own.

Just a few days later, on February 17, 2012, I was reminded of God's protection in the most unexpected way. I had my first job interview lined up, set up by Miss Tanner, the job coordinator, at LD Distributors. I was excited to step into the workforce, but as I prepared for the interview, a man in my dorm—a Muslim man—warned me about the nature of the company. LD Distributors was a pornographic distribution center. Instantly, I knew God was using this man to protect me. I had struggled with pornography in my past, and walking into that environment could have destroyed my testimony and tarnished the work God had done in my life. It was a close call, but God delivered me from that temptation, just as 2 Peter 2:9 says: *The Lord knows how to deliver the godly out of temptation.* I didn't even attend the interview. The enemy had tried to ensnare me, but God had intervened.

Life at the halfway house wasn't without its own set of challenges. On February 21, 2012, I was woken up at 5:15 AM with a flashlight in my face, dragged out of bed to take yet another drug test—the fifth one since arriving. It felt invasive, a constant reminder that the system still saw me as an inmate, not a free man. But through it all, I was reminded of the importance of this season of solitude with God. A woman from my past, someone who had distanced herself from me during my incarceration, had recently reconnected with me. After a difficult conversation, she forgave me for my past actions, and hearing those words from her released a burden I didn't know I was carrying. God's hand was in every moment, teaching me trust, patience, and humility as I awaited full restoration.

February 24, 2012.

That day, I woke with a sense of gratitude. I was still without formal employment, despite my efforts, but God was providing for me in unexpected ways. I had a work detail placement, and I knew it was a sign that God was preparing the way for me. That morning, SJ called. We had been in contact since my release, but the last time I had seen her was in May 2009. She asked if anyone was visiting me the next day, and when I said no, she told me, "Put me down. I'm coming." Her words touched something deep within me. I cared about SJ, and I knew she cared for me. The anticipation of seeing her face-to-face for the first time in years filled me with both excitement and nervousness. God was reconnecting us, and I had to trust His timing in all things.

Later that day, I met with my case manager, Mr. Moore. He informed me that on Monday, I would need to attend a PRJ meeting since I had not yet secured a job. It was disheartening in some ways, but I clung to God's promises. I knew He would provide for me, just as He had during my time in prison. I didn't know how or when, but I trusted that when God's timing was right, He would open the door to meaningful employment. It

Chapter Fourteen

wasn't about the pay—it was about fulfilling the calling God had placed on my life, to be part of a ministry that would bring others out of darkness and into His marvellous light.

Each day, I felt more and more like God was bringing me full circle, from brokenness to restoration. I knew my story wasn't over. The same God who had provided for me during the hardest seasons of my life was the same God who would continue to guide me. With each step I took, each job interview, and each reconnection with the people I loved, I could feel God shaping me for something greater. My journey had just begun, and I was ready to walk wherever He led.

God is in control, no doubt about it. These last few days have been an emotional rollercoaster.

February 25, 2012

One of those days I'll never forget. I saw SJ for the first time in a long while. It was more than just a meeting; it was like our relationship had come full circle. We talked openly, asking for forgiveness, and reflecting on a conversation we had before I was locked up. I told her something I hadn't admitted to many: there were times I didn't feel worthy of the good things God had placed in my life. But now, standing here with her, I realized that God was closing this door. I needed to let go. And I thanked Him for helping me do that.

It felt like closure, but life was far from settled. I had to find work, and, of course, I didn't want to work in another mission—especially after my time at Pacific Garden Mission in Chicago. But sometimes, life has a

The Rebuilding: Second Chance & the Challenge of ReEntry

way of taking you down paths you never expected. I remember grabbing an application for City Union Mission, stuffing it in my backpack, and shaking my head. "No way," I thought, "I'm not working at another rescue mission."

Walking back from Hope Faith Ministries, where they gave me some clothes and a toiletry bag, I passed by City Union Mission. I just stood there, staring at the building, shaking my head again. "No," I thought. "I'll never work at another rescue mission again." But then reality hit. I had my first job interview lined up, and my brother John was there to drive me. I'll never forget his words as he dropped me off, "Go in there, brother, and knock it out." I walked in confidently, my resume polished, shirt and tie looking sharp.

Midway through the interview, the woman interviewing me looked at me and said, "I'm sorry, Mr. Barbee. We can't hire you because you've marked the box as a felon. The company we subcontract with doesn't allow us to hire felons." My heart sank. As I stood to leave, I asked her one last question, "If I weren't a felon, would you have hired me?" She looked at me and said, "With your professionalism and experience, we would've hired you on the spot." I thanked her, and she looked confused. "Why are you thanking me?" she asked. "Because I'm still employable," I told her. And from that moment, I was determined to prove that being a felon wasn't going to define me or my potential.

But the journey wasn't easy. Back at the halfway house, the pressure was mounting. I had been there for over 30 days without a job, and I was getting desperate. Miss Parish, my counselor, wasn't making it any easier.

Chapter Fourteen

I remember her sliding a piece of paper across the desk one day, telling me to sign it. "What's this?" I asked. "I'm writing you up because you're still unemployed," she said, barely hiding her smirk. I tried to explain the obstacles—how hard it was to navigate this city I didn't know, taking buses to interviews for just a few hours each week. But she didn't care. "You've got 30 days to find employment, or we'll send you back to prison," she said.

I felt defeated. I hadn't been written up once in my 44 months of incarceration, but here I was, getting my first write-up in a halfway house. My mind went back to that application from City Union Mission, the one I swore I'd never fill out. But as the days passed, I realized I had no choice. "Okay, Lord," I said, "I'll fill it out." I submitted the application, did a phone screen, and waited anxiously for the next step.

March 3, 2012

Wow, what a roller coaster of emotions this week has been. I've had to remind myself to stay focused. God never said it would be easy, but He promised He would never leave nor forsake me. I'm learning to stand firm on His promises, not get lost in my current circumstances, but to embrace my position in Christ. Yesterday, I felt frustration building up inside as I faced a situation where I needed permission to leave the building, only to be outside for five hours and still under the control of others.

It was a humbling experience. "Lord, forgive me for my impatience. Teach me to wait on You. I need employment—something steady to meet the needs they've set for me here. They'll ease up once I have a job, and I know this is a test of faith. I have to trust that You're working behind the scenes, even when I can't see the results yet."

March 8, 2012
I'm still here at the halfway house, caught in this in-between space. It feels like I'm invisible, like I'm here but not truly seen. Yet, in my spiritual eyes, I know there's movement. I may not have landed a job yet, but I can sense God moving by His Spirit. This week, I made some great connections.

Ricky Peters, a well-connected guy in the community, took me around to fill out job applications. Turns out, he even knows my sister Vicky—the actress! What a small world. My case manager, Mr. Moore, resigned this week. He had a good heart, but I could tell his hands were tied by the system. Even so, I called him yesterday to thank him for all he had done for me. God is aligning people in my path, and for that, I am grateful.

March 9, 2012
Today, my prayer isn't just for a job, but for God's will to be done. If He's leading me to serve there, I'm already thanking Him in advance because I know He will get the glory. Something fresh came to my mind today—CPR.

Not in the traditional sense, but "Christ's Power Restored." That's what I'm clinging to. I'm claiming this as the last time I will be without a job, a home, or a relationship built on true commitment. Looking at where I stand, I know God has a plan, even if it's hard to grasp at the moment. Today, I reconnected with an old friend, Anthony Derek. We've known each other for over 20 years. He and Sharon blessed us with baby gifts when Stephen was born,

Chapter Fourteen

and he has remained a true friend through all my struggles. Lord, I thank You for friends like Anthony, who love unconditionally and stand by me.

March 15, 2012
God is truly in control, and today, I'm holding onto the promise to give thanks in all things, for this is His will for me in Christ Jesus. I'm intentionally choosing an attitude of gratitude today, despite all that's happening. It's a special day—Sherell's birthday. Sixteen years ago, she came into this world, and today, I can't help but marvel at how much she's grown. Early this morning, I shot her a text and sent her a couple of e-cards, celebrating her milestone. It's a bittersweet moment, but I'm grateful that I can still be part of her day in some small way.

On the job front, I've been busy. I've applied for more positions at City Union Mission, and tomorrow, I've got a 20-30 minute phone interview lined up. I'm praying and preparing for it. Lord, You know my deepest desire—to serve in ministry again. I remember the very first days of my incarceration, how You spoke to me so clearly. You said, "The calling on my life was Your business, but my character—that was mine to work on." You've been shaping me, refining me, making sure that my character lines up with the call You've placed on my life.

I'm reflecting on that now, just like I did when you first brought me here to Kansas City. You didn't just bring me here for this moment, or for no reason. You brought me here to serve You, to fulfill the purpose You've always had for me. Just like the times I served You, God at the laundry in Community Corrections of America, in the chapel at Perkins, and during my time in

Forrest City, Arkansas—those moments weren't random. They were all about Your glory. Now, You've placed me here in Kansas City, and I know You have a purpose for me here too.

My life—every challenge, every trial, and every victory—has shaped who I am today. Lord, sometimes I feel like these storms are relentless, but I also know that You allow them because You've placed something powerful inside of me. You're revealing more of it each day, teaching me to stay focused. I'm constantly reminded of the darkness and negativity around me, like today when I caught myself complaining. I quickly had to stop and reflect. If I don't like where I am, I need to remember—it's my own actions that brought me here. Lord, thank You for that humbling reminder, for the blood of Jesus that covers me, and for Your endless forgiveness.

I'm embracing the lessons, trusting that You're working all of this for Your glory. Even here, surrounded by challenges, You're molding me into who I'm meant to be. Thank You, God, for Your grace, Your patience, and for never giving up on me. The journey continues, and I'm ready to keep walking it with You leading the way.

March 17, 2012

The weight of God's plan felt heavy in my heart. I reflected deeply on how **all things work together for good**, even in the face of struggle. Yesterday's phone interview with **Union Mission**, a ministry that serves the homeless in Kansas City, brought a glimmer of hope. I knew that God had placed me here with a purpose: to love and serve this community. I sensed His direction in every moment, trusting that He was orchestrating events

Chapter Fourteen

for His glory.

Just two days prior, on **March 15**, the marshals returned to our RCW (Residential Correctional Facility). This wasn't the first time—they'd been here over 10 times, hauling back men who couldn't abide by the rules. It was a stark reminder of the road I must not travel. Seeing those men taken away, still clinging to their old ways, reminded me of how fragile this path of righteousness is. I vowed to stay on course.

That same day, I spoke with **Keith Sanford**, a friend from over 20 years ago. Our relationship had been strained by the selfishness and damage over your drug usage. On this day, however, we found healing. I asked for forgiveness, and as it often does, forgiveness brought with it a deep sense of peace and release from the pain of the past.

I also read **Isaiah 50:4-10**, which reassured me that even in Babylon, God comforts us. In the midst of this prison-like environment, surrounded by men lost in the darkness, I felt God's presence. The passage urged me to seek Him in all that I do. This place, with all its turnover and negativity, felt oppressive. Men thought they were slick, but the truth is, the game was over—they'd be locked up again quicker than they realized. I prayed that God would fill me with His Holy Spirit, to guide me and keep me on this righteous path.

March 20, 2012

The message was clear: **Be still and know that I am God.** It was hard to be patient, but I needed to stand firm on His promises. My situation was already turning around, and I could feel the glory of God about to manifest. That day, I received a copy of a report that falsely claimed I had met with a job placement official on February 14. I hadn't—I was at the Urban League that day. It was a blatant lie. But then, just as doubt began to creep in, **City Union Mission** called for a second and final interview. God, I knew You were working things out for my good. I trusted You, God, completely. Despite 44 months without a write-up, now with a second one looming, I realized that staying in Your will was the only way forward. It was never about me; it was about You.

March 21, 2012

Then came the call for an in-person interview. I was nervous but hopeful. Gary, the man who interviewed me, stepped out of the room for a moment, and another man named Greg Miller came in. We started talking, and he looked at my resume and said, "I haven't seen that name in a long time." I asked him what he meant, and he replied, "Barbee. Your father wouldn't happen to be Pastor Leo Barbee, would he?" I nodded, and Greg smiled. "I know your dad! I've been to Victory Bible Church a few times. He's a good man."

By the time Gary came back in, it was clear that this wasn't just an interview—it was a divine appointment. They had initially interviewed me for a shelter staff position, but they offered me something even better: a lead shelter manager role. Two days later, they officially offered me the job.

I couldn't believe it. After all the ups and downs, God had opened a door I hadn't even wanted to walk through. But that's how He works sometimes—leading

Chapter Fourteen

us where we need to go, even when it's not where we thought we'd end up. And now, standing at the beginning of this new chapter, I could see that every setback, every no, and every obstacle had led me right here. God was always in control.

March 23, 2012

My quiet time with God led me to **Psalm 80**, where three words spoke to my soul: **Revive, Restore, Return**. First, God had to revive me before He could use me. Then, God restored me. Now, God was preparing to return me to the place He had for me. The day before, I had a powerful interview at City Union Mission. Greg, one of the interviewers, was from Chicago, and Gary had attended **Moody Bible Institute**—both connections affirmed that God's presence was in that room. I felt comfortable sharing my experiences, including my struggles and incarceration. It felt liberating. God was already doing something new, and I praised Him for it.

March 24, 2012

Judith Ann and Shawnda visited me. It had been so long since I'd seen them, but the bond of family remained strong. We reminisced about Uncle Bob, Aunt Star, and our mom. Despite my struggles, love for one another never wavered. My sister **Vicky** and I had been talking daily, and I had been sharing my heart with her, encouraging her to recognize her God-given potential. I knew that our family's trials were also preparing us to make a greater impact for God's kingdom.

March 29, 2012

The goodness of God was undeniable. The job offer from **City Union Mission** came through! I was overwhelmed with gratitude, knowing that God had heard and answered my prayers. Everything was coming full circle—restoration was happening in my life. My pride and sinful ways had driven me so far from God's will, but through it all, He had a purpose for me. The prayers of so many people had carried me, and I knew without a doubt that God's plan for my life was unfolding exactly as it should.

All things truly work together for good to them that love God.

March 30, 2012

As I sat in the quiet of the halfway house, the weight of a new season settled on me like the first rays of dawn after a long, dark night. The memories of my past flickered like scenes in a film—mistakes, moments of grace, and all the twists and turns that led me to this point. The air felt charged with anticipation as I reflected on the blessings God had poured into my life. It was as if I could feel the thread of His purpose woven through every moment, even when I couldn't see it before.

The night before, I looked at my phone and saw an outpouring of love and support from those who had heard the news about my new job at **City Union Mission**. The screen lit up with names that felt like gifts—**Mrs. Harris, Stephen, Sherell, Keith Sanford, Greg Parr, Marie, Jerry, Alfred, Shawnda, Tracy, Ethel, Sam, Aunt Janet**—all these people who had stood with me, rejoiced with me, and believed in me. My heart swelled with gratitude, and I whispered a prayer:

Chapter Fourteen

"**Thank you, Lord**, for the love that surrounds me."

Last week had been a time of attachment and detachment, a pruning of sorts. I had to let go of certain relationships, trusting in God's Word to "stand still and stand on His promises." Those relationships that were unhealthy, that distracted from God's purpose, needed to be released. But now, I could feel new connections forming—new life, new beginnings.

Even as I sat unable to attend church that Sunday, the joy from the day before still lingered. I had been invited to speak at a **Reach Out Street event** at **Grace United Ministries**, and this was my first time sharing my testimony in full since my release from prison just over 70 days ago. Standing there in front of people who didn't know my story, I felt the Holy Spirit guiding my words. I spoke about my imprisonment and how far God had brought me. I used an acronym that had come to me in prayer: **CPR—Christ's Power Restored**. I told them that just like a heart in need of revival, our lives must stay connected to Christ if we are to be restored. That's the only way healing happens.

After the event, I reconnected with **Ms. Lee**, one of the COs from my time at **CCA** (Correctional Corporation of America). She was a Christian and a minister, and we had often talked about faith during my time there. She had always mentioned her praise team ministry, but it wasn't until yesterday that I saw it in action for the first time. Watching her lead, seeing the joy and power of the Spirit in that room, I was reminded of God's faithfulness. From the dark walls of prison to the light of that moment, it felt like I had come full circle.

Another blessing that day was the support of **ST**, a woman who drove in from Topeka just to be with me. I wasn't sure where our relationship was heading—whether it was part of God's plan for me—but I lifted it up to the Lord. "Not my will, but **Your will be done**," I prayed. I knew that whatever came next, God would provide the right person at the right time, a helpmate, a bride, if that was His will. For now, I placed that uncertainty in His hands.

The excitement for what lay ahead was palpable, and I felt like I could touch it. In just a few days, on **April 3, 2012**, I would begin my new position at **City Union Mission**. My heart was filled with both anticipation and humility. I knew this ministry would be different from what I had experienced in Chicago, and I prayed for wisdom. I would be serving people who were broken, lost, and in need of hope, just as I had once been. And I realized that this was my calling—not just a job, but a ministry. God had prepared me for this moment, through every trial and every blessing.

April 3, 2012

Finally, after 73 long days of waiting, praying, and pushing, I gained employment. I couldn't believe it—I was working in Kansas City, Missouri, at City Union Mission. The excitement, the sense of accomplishment, was overwhelming. Every morning, as I signed out of the halfway house, my heart would leap, knowing I was heading to a job where I could serve and grow. The halfway house, though dark and frustrating, didn't break me. Despite the indifference of the staff, I knew the God I serve was bigger than any system or circumstance.

Chapter Fourteen

God truly has a sense of humor, because here I was, in a city where I didn't even know the bus routes, and yet my job was just a 10-block walk from the halfway house. I didn't need to figure out the bus system after all—God made sure I could walk to work, back and forth, each day. City Union Mission knew my situation, knew I was still navigating the residential drug and alcohol aftercare program. Every Wednesday, I had to go back for one hour of outpatient treatment, and the blessing was that they allowed me to stay on the clock during that hour. They knew this was just temporary, and they supported me through it all.

One person I will never forget in this chapter of my journey is Earl Hendrix. He was a godly man at the halfway house who saw beyond my surface, recognizing a deeper calling and brokenness within me. As I shared my story with him, he looked me in the eye and said, "You minister the Gospel, don't you?" I nodded, and he responded, "Allow me to help you be restored." What started as counseling sessions turned into something more—fellowship, mentoring, and genuine support. Earl played a key role in not just my reentry into society but my rededication to Jesus Christ.

Even though I was working 50 to 60 hours a week at City Union Mission, I was excited. This was just the beginning, a transitional phase that would lead to something bigger. God was restoring me, not just to society but back into ministry. What better place to serve than at City Union Mission? I remember the night when Trent Robinson, my supervisor and good friend, came into the office and said, "You've got a message." At first, I didn't understand what he meant, but then he clarified—he wanted me to preach that night because the chapel minister hadn't shown up.

I had little time to prepare, but I felt the Lord leading me to speak from Mark chapter four, about the storm the disciples faced and how Jesus assured them, "We're going to the other side." As I preached to the men that night, something stirred in me. The Holy Spirit nudged me, telling me to show them my storm. So, I pulled up my pants leg, lowered my sock, and revealed the ankle monitor that was tracking my every move, showing them that while I was standing there preaching, I was still in the midst of my storm, right alongside them. The room went silent; you could hear a pin drop. At that moment, the men knew I wasn't just speaking from the pulpit—I was walking through the storm with them.

Opportunities kept unfolding. I connected with the Dismas House through the ATR (Access to Recovery) program, which provided housing vouchers for people with a history of substance abuse. I was eligible, and through God's grace, I found a place at Sober One, a transitional house on Montgall Street. I'll never forget the night I sat down for the interview. They asked me about my substance abuse, my incarceration, and what I believed God was doing in my life. Usually, the men of the house would take a vote and let you know in a few days if you were accepted. But that night was different. Mr. Earl Cobbins looked at me and said, "We're not going to vote. We're placing you in the house."

That moment was another sign of God's hand at work in my life. I had a place to lay my head, and for the next five weeks, I worked at City Union Mission, continued my aftercare, and stayed accountable to both the halfway house and Sober One. Every step of the

Chapter Fourteen

way, God was opening doors, making a way where there seemed to be no way. The excitement of these opportunities filled me with hope, with a fire to keep going, knowing that the storm wasn't the end—God was bringing me to the other side.

The weight of the world felt like a tangible force pressing on my shoulders when I walked into City Union Mission in April 2012. Just months before, I had been confined behind prison walls, grappling with the uncertainty of whether society would ever grant me a second chance. Now, standing at the entrance of this sprawling 300-bed shelter, I was overwhelmed by the sheer magnitude of the task before me. Each bed represented a story—men, women, and children who, like me, had seen their lives shattered and were now grasping for a lifeline. These weren't just numbers or shelter occupants; they were human beings, each carrying emotional, physical, and spiritual wounds, all crying out for healing.

As I took my first steps into the shelter, the familiar echoes of doubt from my past still whispered in my mind. I had been where they were, lost, broken, and searching for purpose. But now, I was here not just to manage the operations of a facility, but to stand on the front lines, battling for the dignity of those who had been forgotten. Every day, I rose before the sun, doing my work clothes like a soldier preparing for battle. The road ahead felt long and treacherous, but I understood that each small victory, each act of compassion, was a step toward reclaiming not only my life, but the lives of those I served.

The responsibility weighed heavily as I navigated through the rows of beds, where many clung to their last thread of hope. I learned to look past the hardened expressions and listen to the unspoken cries for help, seeing the fragility beneath the surface. There were days when I felt pulled in every direction, dealing with emergencies, broken families, addiction, and violence.

Yet, even in the midst of chaos, I found my footing. I worked tirelessly with the staff, setting goals with one purpose in mind: to guide these people toward healing. Sitting in planning meetings, I represented them, speaking as someone who had lived their pain. Each decision we made felt like it had the power to either uplift or crush a soul, and I was determined to choose the former.

As I sat in that halfway house, I could almost feel the shift in the air. It was like a **new beginning**, a fresh wind blowing through my soul, reminding me that God had revived me, restored me, and now He was returning me to the place He had always intended. Every struggle had a purpose. Every tear had watered the soil for the new growth that was now emerging in my life.

"**Lord**," I prayed, "thank You for Your faithfulness. Fill me with Your love, guide me with Your wisdom, and let me be a vessel of Your grace to others." I knew the journey ahead wouldn't be easy, but I was ready to step into this new season, hand in hand with the One who had brought me through it all.

April 4, 2012

I woke up with a heart full of gratitude. The first thought that echoed in my mind was: "**Thank you, Lord, for all you've done in my life.**" I opened my Bible and the words of **Jeremiah 29:11** sprang to life:

Chapter Fourteen

"For I know the plans I have for you," declares the Lord, "plans to prosper you and not to harm you, plans to give you hope and a future." These words, so familiar, had never felt more personal. I could feel the weight of God's plan unfolding before me, like a carefully laid path through the wilderness of my past.

I remember my first full day as **Shelter Manager** at **City Union Mission**, and the significance of it. Just a few months ago, I was in a prison cell, my future clouded with uncertainty. Now, here I was, standing in the very place I knew God had always intended for me—back in ministry, back where I belonged. The joy that welled up inside me was overwhelming. **Boy, what a joy**, I thought, to be back serving the outcast, the broken, the people society had forgotten. This was my calling, my purpose, and I felt it deep in my bones.

Walking through the shelter's halls, I could see the faces of men who had stories not unlike mine—men who had fallen, who had lost their way, and were now seeking redemption. I prayed as I walked: **"Lord, give me wisdom, just as You gave Solomon, to lead these people. Help me to love them as You do, to encourage them, to see them with Your eyes."**

The weight of responsibility felt immense, but so did the peace that came with knowing God had equipped me for this. I asked for more of His wisdom, more of His Spirit to fill me. I knew I couldn't do this on my own. **God has smiled on me today**, I thought, as I moved through the tasks of the day, feeling His favor surround me. I could sense it in the way the staff responded, the way the men in the shelter opened up to me. This was **total restoration**, a moment where the pieces of my life were coming back together, stronger and more purposeful than ever before.

As the day went on, I reflected on how far God had brought me. I was no longer the man who stumbled through life in darkness, driven by selfish desires and sin. God had fought my battles. He had provided for me every step of the way. Now, He has given me a place to live, a ministry to pour myself into, and the strength to do it all through **Christ who strengthens me**.

The enemy tried to plant seeds of doubt—there were challenges at the **halfway house** with the staff, whispers of conflict and tension, but I knew who I was and **whose I was**. I was a child of God, and no matter what came my way, I had the victory. The battle was already won, and I held tight to that truth.

April 5, 2012

I woke up with a renewed sense of joy. **This is the day the Lord has made; I will rejoice and be glad in it.** I had so much to rejoice about—where I had been, where I was now, and where God was leading me. Just four months ago, I was in prison, a place of despair and uncertainty. But today, I was walking in the light of God's purpose, working in ministry again, something I had thought I might never do.

As I stepped into my second day at the mission, I was determined to take my time. There was so much to learn—about the staff, the men we were serving, the rhythm of the shelter—but I felt a calmness, a certainty that God was guiding my every step. **Two or three nights a week**, they told me, I would be the **lead Shelter**

Chapter Fourteen

Manager. It was a heavy responsibility, but I welcomed it. I prayed constantly, "**Lord, help me to stay teachable, help me to be a servant, but most of all, help them to see Jesus in me.**" I didn't want them to see **Leo**; I wanted them to see **Christ** shining through my actions, my words, and my heart.

That afternoon, I lifted up a special prayer for **Brent**. "**Lord, you know him better than I do. You know all his needs, and I ask that You God would meet him where he is.**" Brent had been struggling, and I knew God had the power to restore him, just as He had restored me. As I prayed, my thoughts turned to my own needs—specifically, the desire for a helpmate, a woman who would walk with me in Christ. "**Lord, You know my heart, and I trust You with this. Give me patience to wait on Your God's timing.**" I prayed for a woman who would love me as You love, someone who would have the **mind of Christ** and allow You to be the Lord of our lives together.

As the day drew to a close, I felt an overwhelming sense of peace. **God's Word is true and Amen.** He had brought me this far, and I knew He would continue to guide me in this new season of life. I wasn't just working a job—I was living out a calling, a purpose that had been shaped by every trial, every fall, and every moment of grace in my life. And for that, I was deeply, profoundly grateful.

April 8, 2012

He is Risen Indeed! Today is Resurrection Sunday—a day of renewal, of life conquering death. But for me, it's even more personal. Today, my son Stephen turns 19. The joy of that number isn't lost. I feel the weight of time, of missed birthdays, and the emptiness that comes from being away. Yet today, there's a spark of hope. God is rebuilding the bridge between me and my son, one conversation at a time, one gesture of love after another.

I just got off the phone with Stephen, and hearing his voice fills me with joy I haven't felt in a long time. I've had to learn how to be his friend, to be present from a distance, to offer what I could as his father, even from the confines of where I've been. Each word exchanged between us feels like a stitch in a wound that's slowly healing. There's so much God is doing, even when I don't fully understand it.

I also spoke to Marie, the mother of my children. Even though our journey has been hard and complicated, God's hand is on her, too. I pray for her. I trust that God is watching over her, even when I can't.

As I sit with these thoughts, my mind drifts to work, back to where I began, serving the homeless at the mission. The humble task of serving others, of offering hope to those who seem hopeless, reminds me daily of God's power. This is what it means to die to myself and let Christ live in me. This is how He restores me, piece by piece, to my family and my community. I am a vessel, and through His grace, I continue to grow in favor with God and man.

April 10, 2012

The call of God—it's a powerful thing. It's what drives me to say, *I can do all things through Christ who strengthens me.* The strength I find in Him is the only way I can carry out the tasks set before me. Today, I felt that strength guiding me as I walked into Greg's office. There sat Terence, deep in conversation. They didn't know I would ask, but I mentioned wanting to learn both shifts at work, asking if I could take on the overnight shift.

I thank the Lord for the boldness He's given me to step out in faith, to learn, and to serve wherever I'm needed. This isn't about just covering shifts or filling gaps. It's about walking in obedience, about serving God's people wherever He leads me. Lord, let me continue to serve. Let me reach the lost and be bold for Your kingdom.

April 11, 2012

We wrestle not against flesh and blood, but against principalities, against powers, against the rulers of the darkness of this world.

Today reminded me of that truth more than ever. The enemy uses people, and I see it clearly. My counselor and her negativity and lies were aimed at discouraging me today. She sat there and lied straight to my face about the double shift, but I saw through it. I know the God I serve, and He's already taken control of the situation. This battle isn't mine—it belongs to the Lord, just as it was for Joseph when he was in prison. God has His hand on me even now, and I'm trusting Him to bring glory out of this moment.

Despite the challenges, today was powerful. I had the chance to preach at the mission, and God showed up.

Mark 10:46-50—*come out of darkness*. I spoke those words, and the Holy Spirit moved. Eighteen to twenty men stood up, ready to rededicate their lives to Christ, ready to step into the light. I am in awe of how God uses me. I am His vessel, and He can do with me whatever He pleases.

Later that night, I spoke with SJ—she's really going through it right now, physically, spiritually, emotionally. But I know God is working in her life, just like He's working in mine. I pray for His protection over her. God is good, and He is faithful. I trust Him, even when I can't see the full picture.

April 12, 2012

The Lord made this day, and I will rejoice and be glad in it. Today, I'm reflecting on something the Lord told me a month ago—people connect with me more in my weaknesses, in my struggles, than they ever could through my successes. It's true. My addiction, my homelessness, my imprisonment—these are the things that make me human. These are the things that make me relatable.

At the mission today, a man asked if I had served in the military or if I had been a cop. I laughed and told him "no." When he asked why, I told him my truth—I had been in prison. He was shocked. He couldn't believe it. But that's the power of God. Less than 100 days ago, I was locked up, and now I'm out here, serving and testifying to what He's done.

Later, my coworker Trent came to me, sharing how he, too, had been hired right after imprisonment. He en-

Chapter Fourteen

couraged me, reminding me that we are brothers in this journey. He's walked in my shoes. I'm grateful for these moments of connection, for these reminders that I'm not alone in this path.

April 18, 2012

Ninety days. Today marks ninety days since I've been released from prison. What a day of celebration! I've seen and experienced so much in these three months, and all I can do is give God the glory. Being here in Kansas City, seeing God work—His Word is true.

I remember when Mr. Burns told me I was placed in Kansas City. At first, I was disappointed—I thought I would end up in Leavenworth like most guys from Kansas. But God had a plan. The doors He's opened for me at the Union Mission, the opportunities He's placed before me, all of it is part of His purpose for my life.

It's like the Lord told me: People will identify with your struggles, not your successes. Every day, I see the truth of that statement. My motto is simple—*serve, serve, serve*. Keep serving, no matter what tests come my way.

Today, I'm thankful for the honest man God has made me to become. Just last Sunday, I was in a store and the cashier gave me too much change—an extra $5. I returned it. The man behind me said, "That's an honest man." And I know, back in the day, I wouldn't have done the same. But God has changed me. He's made me new. And for that, I give Him all the glory.

I'm reconnecting with my family, talking more with my sister Vicky and my brother Brian. I'm helping

Brent find work. God is moving in all our lives. Vicky has this opportunity with Lutheran Services, and I know God is going to bless her in ways we can't even imagine. Everything we do is for His glory. Everything. "Thank You, Lord, for all You've done and for all You continue to do. I give You all the praise. Amen."

April 22, 2012

Last night was something else—one of those nights that jolted you back into the reality of where you are. I had just gotten off work and returned to the halfway house, and the place was crawling with US Marshals. Thirty-five, maybe forty of them, combing through every inch of the building. They were checking everything—rooms, belongings—taking away cell phones and anything else that had no business being there. They were serious, making everyone take a breathalyzer and a drug test. The air was thick with tension, and you could feel the unease rising in the room.

As I stood there, watching it all unfold, I felt this nudge inside me. It was God, reminding me: *Remember where you are, and more importantly, remember where you were.* He's brought me out every time, every setback, and every stumble. He's been faithful. And now, whenever I go through something uncomfortable, I hear His voice telling me, *Just don't come back.* It's like He's saying, *Stay on course. Don't lose sight of where I've brought you from.*

There were a lot of complaints from some of the other guys, the ones who had something to hide. My

Chapter Fourteen

mom used to say, "You throw a rock into a pack of dogs, and the one that barks the loudest is the one that got hit." That was last night, for sure. Plenty of barking. But I just kept my head down, focusing on the right things. I know I have to keep trusting God in all things because He is my protector and my provider.

Today was a new day, and God showed up in ways that still leave me in awe. At the City Union Mission, I had the privilege to preach—twice. The first time, at the 2 p.m. service, I shared from *Second Chronicles 13:13-18—Don't lose your shout*. The words flowed, and you could feel the Spirit moving in the room. Men who were weary and broken stood up. Fifteen, maybe eighteen of them, coming forward to restore their lives to God. It was powerful. Watching them stand, I could feel the presence of God—He was working, stirring hearts, and showing His glory.

And then this evening, I had another chance to minister. This time, I came out of *Acts 16:25-31—God still works the midnight shift*. Those words hit home, not just for the men listening but for me too. God works in the dark places, in the middle of our midnight moments. He turns things around when we least expect it. As I spoke, I could feel the weight of my own midnight moments—the times when I thought I was lost, but God turned my situation around for His glory.

After the service, I found myself in a quiet moment of prayer, asking God for direction. I know my time at the halfway house is coming to an end, and I need to know where He wants me to go next. I've been thinking about it a lot—where am I supposed to live? But more than anything, I need His guidance. I don't want to take one step without His guidance. So I prayed: *Lord, not my will, but Your will be done.*

I feel a peace, knowing that God has the next chapter of my life already written. He's brought me this far, and I trust He'll guide me in whatever comes next. Thank You, Lord, for showing up today, for using me as Your vessel. I am in awe of what You are doing, and I will continue to follow wherever You lead.

April 26, 2012

Thank you, Lord, for the call you have placed on my life, a call that is without repentance. I know that *Romans 11:29* is true, and that my struggles, my trials, and everything I've walked through will bring glory to You. Not a day goes by that I don't reflect on Your faithfulness, even when I was faithless. You remained steadfast, holding me in Your grace.

Yesterday, I shared a piece of my story with Mr. Parker, a staff member. It was an old newspaper article from October 2001, and after I handed it back, something broke open in him. He began to share his own struggles with me—how he had once been a pastor and a minister but had been running from his calling. His words resonated with me. We both know the urgency of reaching these young men, the ones who come into the mission, lost and searching for something real.

April 25, 2012

We had a *Lead Shelter Managers* meeting, and after that, I met with Greg Miller. I couldn't keep it in any longer—I shared the burden God placed on my heart. I told him we need a program that will empower

Chapter Fourteen

these young men, a program that will call them to be the men of God they were created to be. *Valor Men*—that's the name that came to me last night. Valid, victorious, abundant living through obedience and restoration. I see the purpose, the pattern, the plan, and the preparation all coming together. Lord, I need You to guide me through this. This is bigger than me—*Your will be done.*

Today, I met a young man named Anthony Jones. He's hurting deeply because of his divorce, and when he opened up, I told him I understood. I've been there. I know what it's like to feel like your world is falling apart because of brokenness. Men like Anthony they're hurting because of their life experiences, and they don't know how to overcome without going under. The enemy tricks us into thinking, *I can do this by myself. I don't need anyone's help.* But that's just pride. Lord, continue to break me, so You can use me. So many men have crossed my path—Kevin, Chris, David, Richard, Danny, Anthony—the list just keeps growing. Each one has a story, and each one needs You.

Lord, *fill me with Your Holy Spirit.* Break me, melt me, mold me, and fill me—this is my prayer. Life in the halfway house is getting easier now that I'm working more. I'm not here much—just to eat and sleep. But as my time winds down, I find myself wondering, *Lord, where do You want me next? Where will I lay my head once my time is up here?* I trust You with all of it—my finances, my job, my ministry, my relationships. God, You know what I need. And Lord, when it comes to a bride, prepare her, in Jesus' name.

May 1, 2012

The Rebuilding: Second Chance & the Challenge of ReEntry

A new day and a new month. Lord, I want to thank You for everything You're doing in my life. This journey is all about You. What a week it's been! Last week, a father named Mr. Tillman came to the mission, searching for his son. As he shared his heart with me, I felt the Spirit move. I told him that his love for his son was an action—it was seen in how he came all this way just to seek him out. I told him to rejoice because his prayers were being answered—his prodigal son was on his way home. As I spoke, I realized I, too, am a prodigal. We prayed together, standing in the gap for his son, knowing that God was working.

In that moment, I knew even more clearly the mandate You've placed on me, Lord. I'm here in Kansas City to *live* the Word of God, to *speak* the Word of God, and to declare that Your Word brings deliverance in any situation. Just last week, a couple came to the mission from Kansas City. They had walked from the bus station, broke and hungry, just looking for something to eat. Mike, the husband, was sick and bleeding. Seeing him, I was led to pray for him—for his healing before they reached Pennsylvania, for provision, and for protection over his wife Karen and their family.

May 6, 2012

I preached again, this time from *John chapter 9*. The Spirit of God was so present, and once again, about 15 men stood up for restoration and re-dedication. Lord, I don't want to be anywhere except in Your will. Yesterday, I went for an interview at the *Sober One House*—a transitional home. I felt good about what they stand for, but I know I need to keep seeking You. *Is this where You want me, Lord?* I lay it all before You. Guide me in

Chapter Fourteen

Jesus' name. Amen.

May 9, 2012

Wow, Lord, what a week! You keep showing me Your power and presence every single day. I'm more aware than ever of the *Kingdom of God* and the *kingdom of darkness* constantly at work around me. I know I need to seek Your face daily, to hear Your voice clearly, and to obey. Your will is all I want, Lord. Help me to stay filled with Your Spirit, to be led by Your Spirit, to serve You with all I am. More of You, Lord, and less of me.

Every day is an opportunity to touch someone's life. Just today, I met a man named David. After doing his intake, I felt led to encourage him and pray with him. And last Friday, I had the chance to meet a young man named Brian. He came to the mission just to charge his phone, but You had a different charge in mind. As I shook his hand, I told him it was a blessing to be able to do so because not long ago, I couldn't. Just over 120 days ago, I was still in prison, but now, You've set me free. I told him how You've turned my life around. Lord, thank You for my imprisonment because it's brought glory to You.

I don't want people to know my name—I want them to see *Your God characteristics* in me. A man of God. That's what they keep saying—*I see the light in your face. I see God's glory all over you.* And it's true, Lord. You've transformed me, and I am so thankful.

As I look ahead, I leave my living situation in Your hands, trusting that You know exactly where I need to be. Serving at the mission has been a blessing, and I'm so grateful for the opportunities You've given me to bring You glory. I know now that staying ready means not having to get ready. In every season, in and out of season, I'm here, Lord—*use me until You use me up*. Amen.

May 13, 2012

Today, as the sun rose over Kansas City, God's plans and purposes felt more tangible than ever. I could sense the Spirit moving, urging me to lean into His will, not mine. There's always that struggle, that constant reminder that I must surrender daily, asking, "Lord, not my will, but Yours be done."

Why do I feel this so strongly today? A man I hadn't seen since 1997, when I served at Pacific Garden Mission, crossed my path. Back then, he was part of the program, trying to piece his life together like so many others who had found themselves at the mission. And here he was again, years later, right here in Kansas City.

I had been in conversation with a staff member, reminiscing about how we used to operate at Pacific Garden Mission—how we would emphasize the need to spiritually "get dressed" every day, putting on the armor of God. As I was talking, this man—this same man from 1997 began quoting Ephesians 6:10-18 right in front of me. His words stirred something deep within me, bringing tears to my eyes.

It felt like a divine moment. All those years ago, I would remind the men daily to clothe themselves in the armor of God: truth, righteousness, peace, faith, salvation, the Word, and prayer. And here was living proof that the seeds planted back then had not fallen on barren

Chapter Fourteen

soil. God's faithfulness was on full display. It wasn't just a memory from the past; it was evidence that my labor had not been in vain.

"Lord, I can't, but You can," I whispered. "All I desire is to do Your will." The path is clearer now. I see things, though still dimly, and I long to hear Your voice more clearly—speak when You tell me to speak, and remain silent when You tell me to be still. As Your Spirit moves, I want to move with You, in step with Your timing. Thank You, Lord, for the people You've allowed me to help today, like Tracy, Ken, and Alan. Let me continue to be Your hands and feet.

The spiritual battle I face daily reminds me to stay anchored in Your Word. It breaks me, humbles me, and then fills me anew. My prayer remains the same: Lord, increase Your presence in me, let Your Holy Spirit overflow.

May 15, 2012

Yesterday wasn't an easy day. I had prayed for God to reveal anything hidden, and sure enough, He answered in ways I didn't expect. It was supposed to be a day off, and I spent time with SJ, just driving around town, enjoying a break from the routine. We went to the park, had some laughs, and for a moment, I thought everything was fine.

When she dropped me off back at the halfway house, she left something behind—a cigarette pack in my pocket. I didn't think much of it and was about to throw it away when my phone rang. It was SJ. She asked if I still had the pack and said there was something inside it.

Confused, I checked, and my heart sank. It wasn't just cigarettes. Hidden inside were drugs.

I knew in that instant that our relationship was over. If the staff had found those drugs on me, I could have easily been looking at another five to ten years. I thanked the Lord right then and there for protecting me. I could have lost everything. I texted SJ, "Thanks for nothing," and though she apologized, I felt a deeper truth had been revealed. What was hidden had been exposed. And I forgave her, not for her sake, but because I knew that holding onto bitterness would only hinder me from moving forward. God's hand was in it all, even in the painful end of that relationship.

May 22, 2012

God is in control. That's the truth I cling to every day, especially now. I've got just seven weeks left at this halfway house, and the spiritual battle seems to be intensifying. The enemy is busy, stirring up confusion, division, and deceit. But I've learned to seek God in all that I do, not to travel down the deceptive paths that might lead me away from Him.

I'm reminded not to seek the approval of man but to be a servant of God. "Lord, let me hear Your voice, let me see Your hand in all things, and let me wait upon You," I prayed today. There's a lot of noise around me—the hustle and bustle of the mission, the men struggling to grow in their faith. It can be discouraging at times. I don't always see the level of commitment I hope for in these programs, but I remind myself that transformation takes time.

Chapter Fourteen

As I reflect on my sermon from last Sunday, I remember the truth I shared from Revelation 12:10-12. We overcome life's challenges by the Word of God and by the testimony of our lives. That truth resonates deeply with me as I push through these last weeks. The enemy may be working hard, but God is in control. I see the evil in the hearts of men around me, but I refuse to let that discourage me. Instead, I focus on the victory I have in Christ.

The small stuff—arguments with staff, frustrations with those I live with—it's all just noise. I won't let it distract me from the bigger picture. Thank You, Lord, for protecting me, guiding me, and giving me the opportunity to minister to these men. Let me stay focused, stay humble, and stay in step with Your Spirit, trusting You for what lies ahead.

May 24, 2012

The day started like many others at City Union Mission—men arriving with their burdens, seeking refuge, some weary and broken, others quietly hoping for a change. As I walked through the familiar halls of the mission, the weight of my past and the magnitude of God's grace felt especially close.

"Thank you, Lord," I whispered as I reflected on Romans 7:21-25, the passage I had just shared with the men in our Bible study. It was a scripture that resonated deeply, capturing the struggle between the desire to do good and the ever-present pull of sin. I could see in their faces as I spoke that they knew this struggle well. We all do. But the beauty of it is that Jesus has already won the battle for us.

Later that day, I found myself sitting with Steve Gavin, patiently showing him how to navigate the Bible. It wasn't just about teaching him how to find chapters and verses; it was about opening a door to a relationship with God through His Word. Steve's eyes lit up as he began to understand, and I thanked God for using me in that moment.

But the day wasn't over yet. As I made my way through the busy mission, a face from my past stopped me in my tracks. I recognized him immediately, even though it had been almost a decade. "Is your name Cuba?" I asked. He turned, surprised, and nodded. I reminded him of who I was—how he had sold me crack back in 2003.

He looked at me, shocked at the sudden connection, then smiled. "That was a long time ago," he said, "I don't do that anymore."

We both stood there for a moment, the weight of our shared history hanging between us. Then, in that hallway, surrounded by the echoes of men struggling to find hope, we embraced. It was more than just a hug—it was a testament to God's redeeming power. The past had walked into my present to show me just how far God had brought me. I stood there, overwhelmed by gratitude. "Thank you, Lord," I whispered. "You are so awesome."

May 26, 2012

The sun peeked through the windows of the mission as I prepared for another day. "Thank you, Lord, for another day to worship and serve You," I prayed, reflecting on the immense privilege of using the gifts God

Chapter Fourteen

had given me. Serving these men at City Union Mission wasn't just a job—it was a calling, a chance to shepherd, to guide, and to be an example of Christ's love.

Today, I knew I had to be especially sensitive to the Holy Spirit. It's not always easy to discern the spiritual battles these men face—the kingdom of light versus the kingdom of darkness is at war every day. But I knew that, filled with the Holy Spirit, I could stand firm. My desire was simple: to be Christ-like, to stand on the Word of God, and to turn every encounter into a teachable moment.

One of the women I encountered recently, Vicki, had been going through so much. But today, I felt a shift. God was getting ready to shower her with blessings, to turn her trials into a testimony. I reminded her that when we go through hard times, we can often see the hand of God more clearly afterward. He knows our needs and desires, and His timing is perfect. I told her to trust that God was preparing something good for her, even if she couldn't see it yet. "He's in control," I assured her.

June 3, 2012

"This is the day the Lord has made," I declared as I opened my Bible, feeling a surge of energy and excitement. Today, I had the privilege of sharing the Word of God with the men at the mission. The scripture that came to my heart was Exodus 14:10-18, a powerful passage about coming up out of Egypt, out of bondage, and into freedom.

As I preached, I could feel the Holy Spirit moving through the room. The message wasn't just about ancient

The Rebuilding: Second Chance & the Challenge of ReEntry

Israelites—it was about every man sitting in front of me. It was about coming up out of their personal Egypt, the places of addiction, sin, and despair. I reminded them that the love of God covers a multitude of sins, and that no matter how far they had wandered, God's love could bring them back.

After the message, one of the men, Richard Miller, approached me with tears in his eyes. Just the night before, I had asked him to leave because he had been drinking, and now here he was, humbled and repentant. "I've heard a lot of messages," he said, "but the one tonight touched me. God touched me."

I smiled, seeing the transformation happening right before my eyes. "He recognized his Egypt," I thought to myself, thanking God for allowing me to witness these moments of breakthrough.

Not long after, another man, JB, came up to me. His story was one I had heard many times—caught in a cycle of old friends, old habits, drinking, and smoking crack. "I'm tired," he said, his voice heavy with the weight of it all. "The message touched me, too. But really, God touched me."

It was these moments, these raw, real encounters with God's power, that kept me going. Each day at the mission brought new challenges, but also new victories. I was reminded once again that this was all about God's work, not mine.

And then, as if to put a divine exclamation point on the day, I thought back to Friday. My dad had called me, needing some money. A year ago, I couldn't have

Chapter Fourteen

helped him. But today, I was in a position to give, and I felt the weight of that blessing. I handed the money over without hesitation, telling him, "It's a blessing to give." God had brought me so far, and now, He was using me to be a blessing to others.

That same Friday, my son Stephen came to visit. It was only the third time I had seen him since getting out of prison, and the 40 or so minutes we spent together felt like a precious gift. I showed him around my job, proud of where God had placed me.

Yesterday, as I was heading to work, I overheard a woman on a payphone saying she needed $100. I didn't have the full amount, but I felt the Holy Spirit nudging me. I walked a few feet away, but then I stopped. "Go back," the Spirit whispered. So, I turned around and gave her what I had. It wasn't much, but it was something.

In that moment, I realized something: it's not just about hearing God's voice—it's about obeying it. And every act of obedience, no matter how small, brings us closer to the heart of God.

June 7, 2012

The morning light filtered through the window of the halfway house as I sat in quiet reflection, staring out at the city beyond. "Your will be done today, Lord," I prayed softly. I could feel God's presence, a constant reminder that I wasn't alone in this journey. Over the past week, He had been revealing to me a powerful principle—one that defines the very essence of His Kingdom: to give, and give, and keep on giving.

"For God so loved the world that He gave..." Those

The Rebuilding: Second Chance & the Challenge of ReEntry words echoed in my heart. In just the past few days, I had been tested in this very area. My dad called on Tuesday and again on Friday, in need of help. Without hesitation, I gave him $250. On Saturday, as I walked to work, I overheard a young woman on the payphone, her voice filled with desperation. Without even thinking, I approached her and gave her $10. Then on Monday, Vicki reached out, and I gave her $100. By Wednesday, Tasha had texted me needing $25, and again, I gave.

It wasn't about the money—it never is. It was about being a vessel, a conduit for God's blessings to flow through. It was about letting go of the notion that I had to hold on tightly to what I had. God had placed me in these situations to be a blessing, to reflect His generosity. And now, as I sat there, reflecting on it all, I realized that every act of giving wasn't just for them—it was shaping me, molding me into the man God had called me to be.

I was also filled with gratitude. Just this past week, I had been approved for home confinement. "Praise the Lord," I whispered, feeling a rush of relief. As I sat by the window, looking out at the world beyond the halfway house, I thanked God for His favor, for His presence, and for His power in my life. "Lord, I need more of You," I prayed. "Let Your will be done, and let those I come in contact with see Jesus in me."

The spiritual warfare around me was real, the darkness tangible, but I wasn't afraid. God's Word promised that I didn't have to fear because He was with me. "By His stripes, I am healed," I declared, pleading the blood of Jesus over my life and the lives of those around me. The enemy was busy, but God had given me authority, and I would stand firm in that truth. Amen.

Chapter Fourteen

June 8, 2012

Today, God used broken pieces to reveal His grace once again. As I made my way to the mission, I noticed a man sitting on the sidewalk outside, his head hung low, shoulders slumped in defeat. Something about his posture tugged at my heart. I approached him slowly and asked, "Is everything alright?"

He looked up, his eyes heavy with sorrow. "No," he muttered. I could see the weight of his struggles etched across his face.

"Can I pray for you?" I asked gently. He nodded, and right there, on the sidewalk, I placed my hand on his shoulder and began to pray—for him, for his children, for the restoration of his family. His kids were in the system, and he had no idea where they were. As I spoke the words aloud, I could feel his pain, his longing to be reunited with them. I prayed that God would make a way where there seemed to be none.

Later that morning, I saw him again, this time standing with a friend. I approached him once more, and we prayed again, lifting up his children and his situation to God. As we finished, another young man, Johnny, stood nearby, watching us. He hesitated for a moment, then stepped forward. "Sir, could you pray with me too?" he asked, his voice barely above a whisper.

My heart ached for him. He told me that no one had ever prayed for him or with him before. We prayed together right there, and he opened up to me. Johnny was only 22, fresh out of prison as of January 2012, and already he felt lost, unsure of where to go or how to avoid the same pitfalls that had trapped him before. I shared my story with him, telling him about my own struggles, my own journey out of darkness. He looked at me, his eyes filled with hope, and asked, "Can you help me? I don't want to go down the wrong path again."

"Oh Lord," I prayed silently, "today is a day of expectation. Let me see Your glory." Amen.

June 21, 2012

So much has happened since my last entry, and I can only say, "Thank You, Lord." Today, I'm writing from Sober One House, having moved out of RCC on June 19th. Though I'm still accountable to them, I'm thankful to be away from most of the negativity that surrounded me there. I feel lighter, freer, and more determined than ever to let God's light shine in me.

Last Sunday was Father's Day, and I had the privilege of sharing a message with the men at the mission. "Give your way out of your situation," I told them, speaking from my own experience. God had been teaching me so much about giving—not just material things, but giving of myself, my time, my heart.

As I walked back to RCC later that day, I noticed a young woman sitting on the curb, tears streaming down her face. I approached her, offering a simple message: "You know, Jesus loves you." She looked up, startled, and then the tears came harder. We talked for a while, and I prayed with her. As I turned to leave, the Lord spoke to me again: "Give her some money."

I didn't hesitate. I gave her what I had, knowing that it wasn't about the amount—it was about obedience.

Chapter Fourteen

Every opportunity to give was an opportunity to be a blessing. And I knew, deep in my heart, that God was opening doors and pouring out His wonders in my life.

"Humble yourself under the hand of God, and He will exalt you in due time," I reminded myself as I walked away. My due time was coming. God had brought me too far for me to go back now. I needed His wisdom and His guidance more than ever, especially in these final weeks.

This week, I sent two letters to Jeff, along with some money. I know how he feels, and I pray that God watches over him as he navigates his own struggles. I want to have a heart that serves, to be a vessel that brings God glory, and to pray without ceasing—for my coworkers, for the men at City Union Mission, for everyone God brings into my life.

God's provision never ceases to amaze me. Just the other day, Vicki came by, frustrated because her car had broken down. She took it to the dealership, bracing for a hefty repair bill. But in a moment of divine intervention, they charged her only $50 to fix it—no charge for labor. "Look at God," I marveled. He truly does open the windows of heaven and pour out blessings in ways we can't even imagine.

And so, I keep pressing forward, eyes fixed on Him, trusting that the best is yet to come.

June 29, 2012

"Glory to God," I whispered, staring out the small window of the halfway house, watching the world outside move on, oblivious to the journey I was on. Two weeks ago, I walked out of RCC for the last time. The place had its challenges, yes, but it gave me structure, accountability—things I desperately needed. Still, my flesh had moments of frustration. I would feel the walls closing in, my freedom so near yet still out of reach. But in my spirit, there was joy. A deep, unshakable joy, knowing that God's hand was on my life, guiding me through every storm, every moment of doubt.

This week, in particular, had been good. Monday was a blessing. Dad came down to visit, and we spent the day together—shopping, laughing, just being father and son. It wasn't so much about the things we bought, but about the connection, the fellowship. These moments were rare, and I treasured every second. As the sun began to set, I thanked God for the time, for the healing that had taken place in our relationship.

Later that day, I had a counseling session with Miss Easley. When I arrived, I could tell she wasn't feeling well, so instead of diving into our usual discussions, we just talked. Sometimes, talking was more therapeutic than structured counseling. As we spoke, I felt a nudge in my spirit. The Lord was telling me to pray for someone. On my way back to the halfway house, I sat on the bus and saw a woman with an oxygen tank. "Is she the one, Lord?" I wondered. But no, it wasn't her.

When I got back to Miss Easley, we spoke about the attacks of Satan, how the enemy always seems to strike hardest when God is preparing to bless us or use us. She shared with me about her new position, how she was leaving RCC, stepping into a new chapter that she felt was her true calling, her purpose. Then, she asked me to pray for her. At that moment, I knew she was the

Chapter Fourteen

one God had put on my heart to pray for. We bowed our heads together, and I lifted her up to the Lord, asking for guidance, protection, and favor in her new journey.

Chapter FIFTEEN

FREEDOM AND RENEWAL

July 6, 2012

Today was a milestone—a day I had been waiting for. My last day accountable to the halfway house in Kansas City, Missouri. I packed my things and moved in with my sister Vicki. It's been a blessing reconnecting with her, laughing together, and rediscovering our bond as siblings. We've had time to sit and talk, to catch up on years that felt lost, and to experience God's healing and restoration in our relationship.

This past week has been filled with opportunities, ones that I know God is orchestrating. Last Friday, I had the chance to preach the Word of God at St. Stephen's Baptist Church here in Kansas City. It was a powerful moment, standing in front of the congregation, feeling the Spirit move through me as I shared His Word. And next Sunday, I'll be preaching at Grace United Community Ministries, a place that serves the down and out—

Chapter Fifteen

the homeless, the drug addicts, the ones society often overlooks.

Vicky's friend, Greg Parr, mentioned that the current pastor, Reverend Garfield, is stepping down, and Greg told Vicky that he plans to recommend me for the position. I was stunned, humbled, and a little anxious. "God, not my will, but Yours be done," I prayed. I know that my heart's desire is to pastor, to shepherd God's people, but I also know that every experience, every trial, is preparation for something greater. I trust that God is at work, even when I can't see the full picture.

July 8, 2012

This past week has been filled with opportunities, ones that I know God is orchestrating. Last Friday, I had the chance to preach the Word of God at St. Stephen's Baptist Church here in Kansas City. It was a powerful moment, standing in front of the congregation, feeling the Spirit move through me as I shared His Word. And next Sunday, I'll be preaching at Grace United Community Ministries, a place that serves the down and out—the homeless, the drug addicts, the ones society often overlooks.

Vicky's friend, Greg Parr, mentioned that the current pastor, Reverend Garfield, is stepping down, and Greg told Vicky that he plans to recommend me for the position. I was stunned, humbled, and a little anxious. "God, not my will, but Yours be done," I prayed. I know that my heart's desire is to pastor, to shepherd God's people, but I also know that every experience, every trial, is preparation for something greater. I trust that God is at work, even when I can't see the full picture.

Today, I preached at Victory Bible Church in Lawrence, Kansas, and it was a day I will never forget. The message was about the power of forgiveness and restoration, and as I stood before the congregation, some of whom I had wronged in the past, I felt a deep sense of healing. These were people I had lied to, disrespected, and hurt. But today, they embraced me with grace. The elders and leaders laid hands on me, praying for my continued growth and restoration. "Wow, God, You are truly a forgiving God," I thought as tears filled my eyes.

After the service, I spent time with my family—sisters, brothers, daughters, nieces, and nephews. We laughed, we cried, and we marveled at God's faithfulness. To stand here, to be able to look them in the eyes, knowing that I had hurt them in the past but was now restored—it was a moment of overwhelming gratitude. God had taken the broken pieces of my life and put them back together, not as they were before, but stronger, better, and I was more whole for it.

I still don't fully understand what God is doing, but I trust Him. He's up to something bigger and greater than I could ever imagine. And all I can say is, "Thank You, Lord, for all that You've done and continue to do in my life." Amen.

July 13, 2012

Today was a milestone—a day I had been waiting for. My last day accountable to the halfway house in Kansas City, Missouri. I packed my things and moved in with my sister Vicki. It's been a blessing reconnecting with her, laughing together, and rediscovering our bond as siblings. We've had time to sit and talk, to catch up on

Chapter Fifteen

years that felt lost, and to experience God's healing and restoration in our relationship.

Today marked a new chapter in my life, a day of profound freedom. I remember it vividly because it was the day I could finally cut the leg monitor off. No longer tethered to the halfway house, no longer held accountable in any form to that system. It was the start of my true return to life outside, and I could feel the weight of those chains being lifted as I walked out the door.

My sister had driven me to the halfway house that morning. We returned the black box that had been strapped to my ankle, and as we walked back to the car, she handed me a small box. "Happy Birthday, Brother," she said with a smile. I opened the box, and inside was a key. She looked at me and said, "You can move in with me."

I was stunned. That key—it wasn't just a piece of metal. It was my first birthday gift after being released from prison, and it symbolized so much more. It meant trust, a chance, and the beginning of something new. Moving from the transitional house to live with my sister in Kansas City was a blessing beyond words. I settled into her place on 84th Street Terrace, and it was a huge step toward stability. Every day, I'd catch the bus from there to work, sometimes late into the night, coming home exhausted but grateful.

God always provides what you need, and one day, standing at the bus stop late at night, that provision came in the form of a coworker. Pat Kelley, one of the guys I worked with at City Union Mission, saw me waiting for the bus. He pulled over and asked, "Where are you headed?"

"South," I told him, trying not to sound too tired. Without hesitation, Pat said, "Get in."

From that night forward, Pat made sure I got home safe. He didn't have to do it, but he did, and that's just one of the ways God was showing up in my life.

Working at City Union Mission was more than just a job—it was my calling at the time. Fresh out of prison, I was surrounded by men who were where I had been—broken, hurting, battling addiction. It was a constant reminder of what God had pulled me out of. I wasn't homeless anymore, I wasn't drowning in drugs or alcohol, and because of that, I was able to serve these men with real compassion and empathy. I saw myself in them.

There was one night I'll never forget. A man came into the shelter, clearly under the influence. His eyes were glazed over, his movements sluggish. I looked at him and asked gently, "Have you been drinking?" He shot back defensively, "There you go, judging me."

But I wasn't judging him. I saw the old me in him. I knew that pain, the disappointment, the shame. I said, "I'm not judging you. I just know what you're going through, because I've been there." He looked at me differently after that. I told him he could stay, as long as he didn't cause any trouble.

There were many men like him—men I met, men who thought I was helping them, but they were helping me just as much. One of those men was Thomas Graves. He called from Leavenworth, saying he needed a place to stay. When he showed up that night, he was drunk, and

Chapter Fifteen

the rules were clear—I couldn't let him in. So I directed him to the bus station just a block away.

I felt awful, but rules were rules. The next day, Thomas came back, sober and thankful. He told me that being turned away had been the wake-up call he needed. He eventually joined the Christian Life Program at the mission, completed it, and later started his own ministry, *Shining for Jesus.* Every time I think about Thomas, I remember how God's plan is always at work, even when we don't see it.

When my time at City Union Mission came to an end, it wasn't because I wanted to leave, but because a new opportunity opened up. I started working part-time at Open Options, a home healthcare facility, while still working full-time at the mission. Balancing both was tough, but I made it work, hustling to make ends meet. Then, an opportunity for a full-time coordinator position opened at Open Options. I applied, figuring it might be time for a change, and I got the job. Now, I was overseeing three houses, with a staff of about 25 and a clientele of 10 individuals.

It was a step up, no doubt about it. But sometimes when you walk through an open door, it isn't God's door. Looking back, I realized maybe this wasn't where He wanted me to be long-term. But I walked through that door anyway, thinking it was the next logical step. Soon enough, things shifted, and God closed that door.

Yet even as one chapter ended, I knew another one was beginning. Every closed door leads to new opportunities, and I have learned to trust that God's timing is perfect—even when I don't understand it. I'll never forget the moment I first asked my probation officer about the possibility of getting off parole early.

I had been out of prison for over two years by then, my release date burned into my memory: January 18, 2012. Sixty months of post-release supervision loomed large over me like a shadow that refused to fade. My probation officer—well, she wasn't unkind, but she was cautious. "Give it more time," she told me, her voice gentle but firm. "You're doing a lot of things right, Stephen. But just wait a little longer."

Her words hung in the air, but deep inside, something stirred. I knew I had been doing the work—not just the surface-level stuff, but the hard, soul-searching kind. And I was starting to hear a voice much stronger than the caution in hers. It was the voice of God, guiding me, pushing me toward freedom, toward release. I had to trust that voice, even when it didn't make sense to others.

One day, in what felt like an act of faith, I picked up the phone and dialed the Federal Probation Public Defender's Office. When Shay Ramsey answered, her voice steady and professional, she asked me point-blank: "Why do you think you should be off paper early?" I took a deep breath, heart pounding, and told her the truth. I wasn't just skating by. Since my release, I have stayed clean—no drugs, no law-breaking. I had been employed since April of 2012, and not just employed, but thriving.

In 2013, I got a promotion at my job! I had paid off my court fines. I was living right, walking straight, and doing everything the system asked of me. I could feel Shay listening closely on the other end, weighing my words, feeling the weight of my journey. She told me

Chapter Fifteen

she'd reach out to my probation officer to get a sense of who I was from her perspective.

I'll never forget the day Shay called me back, her voice full of quiet certainty. "Your probation officer said you've been a model client. No issues, no problems. I'm going to file the petition for your early release," she said. "Now, this could take a while—maybe two, three, even four months before we get a court date." But I knew in my heart—when God moves, He moves fast. Sure enough, just one week later, Shay called again. "Stephen," she said, "we've got court this week."

I walked back into the same courtroom where, years earlier, I had stood shackled before the judge, waiting for my 70-month federal prison sentence to drop like a hammer. The same prosecutor, the same judge, even the detective who had built the case against me—every face was the same, like a snapshot from my past, only this time the air was different. I wasn't the man who had stood there before. I was changed, redeemed, and God was with me.

When the prosecutor stood to speak, his words felt sharp, intended to wound. "Stephen Barbee is a menace to society," he said, his voice cutting through the room. "He has not done everything we asked." My heart pounded, but before I could even react, Judge Lungstrom leaned forward, his voice carrying authority. "If you don't have anything concrete against this man, I'm telling you to sit down." The prosecutor's words crumbled in the air, and he sat down, defeated.

Then it was Shay's turn. She spoke with conviction, laying out every fact—no positive random urin analysis, steady employment, fines paid in full. She painted a picture of a man who had done more than was required, a man who had worked hard for redemption. She spoke about my growth, my commitment, and my readiness to step fully into a new chapter.

And then, the words that will forever be etched in my soul: "The case of the United States of America versus Stephen Barbee is officially closed."

March 3, 2014

The weight of those words, the finality of it, crashed over me like a wave. I walked out of that courthouse, my vision blurred by tears, my heart pounding with gratitude. My dad and stepmother, Mrs. Helen, were waiting for me outside. As soon as I stepped out, they wrapped me in their arms, their warmth pressing into me like a blanket of love and relief. "God is good," my dad whispered.

I cried. Tears of release, tears of joy, tears of knowing that God had orchestrated every step of this journey. He had been with me through every trial, every victory, every moment of doubt. And as 2014 unfolded, I knew that this was just the beginning. God wasn't finished. He had more to do, more blessings to bestow, and more paths for me to walk.

Chapter Fifteen

Chapter SIXTEEN

FINDING HOPE THROUGH FAITH

In June of that year, I found myself in a dark place. I had just lost my job at Open Options, and the weight of unemployment hit me like a ton of bricks. Each day seemed like an endless loop of doubt and despair, with no clear way forward. I remember the suffocating feeling that gnawed at my spirit, the way the walls of my home felt like they were closing in, and one afternoon, I couldn't bear it anymore. I grabbed my car keys, got into my car, and just drove. I needed to escape, even if it was just for a little while.

I didn't have a destination in mind; I just followed the road, hoping somehow that movement would calm the chaos in my mind. I turned onto a familiar street, and as I passed by an old firehouse, something caught my eye. A sign hung from the building: *Metro Lutheran Ministries*. It was a place I had never thought much of,

Chapter Sixteen

but for some reason, it stood out that day.

I kept driving. A few blocks passed by, and then, as clear as if someone was sitting beside me, I heard it—*the voice of God*. He said, *"Go in."* I shook my head, trying to ignore it, thinking maybe it was just my mind playing tricks on me. But the voice came again, stronger this time: *"Now."*

Something inside me stirred, and before I knew it, I had turned the car around. I didn't know why or what I was walking into, but I pulled up in front of that firehouse, stepped out, and approached the building. When I opened the door and walked into the reception area, it felt surreal. My voice seemed distant as I asked the receptionist a simple question: *"Are you hiring?"*

She made a call upstairs to the executive director, but the answer was disappointing. "No, not right now," she said. "But if any positions open up, we usually post them on NP Connect."

I left with a mix of hope and frustration, feeling like I had taken a step of faith, only for it to lead to a dead end. When I got home, I decided to check my LinkedIn account, and there it was—Jim Glynn's picture. I had connected with him on the platform a while back, so I sent him a message. To my surprise, he quickly replied, saying he had heard I had been in the building that day and wished me success in my job search.

The very next day, I went on NP Connect, and wouldn't you know it—there was an opening at Metro Lutheran Ministries for their Learning to Earn Program. It was for the role of Program Coordinator. My heart skipped a beat. I wasted no time; I sent in my cover letter and resume immediately.

Two weeks passed before I received a phone call from a young man named Jacob Bosch. He asked if I was still interested in the position. Of course, I was! A week later, I found myself sitting across from Jacob in my first interview. As I shared my professional experience, I also felt compelled to be honest about my past—about my incarceration and the obstacles I had faced. Jacob listened intently, his eyes never leaving mine. After a long pause, he finally said, *"I've never met anyone like you. You're quite interesting... but unusual."*

He told me he needed to consult with the executive director, but something in his tone gave me hope. The next day, he called to set up a second interview. This time, it was with both Jacob and Jim Glynn. We sat down for what felt like an hour-long conversation. As the interview wrapped up, Jim looked at me with a curious expression. He asked, *"There's a pastor in Lawrence, Kansas, with the same last name as yours. He's well-known and respected. Is that your father?"*

I smiled and nodded, "Yes, that's my father."

Jim leaned back, his face thoughtful. *"You know, you could've walked in here riding on your father's coattails. But you didn't. You came here on your own character, your own integrity. That speaks volumes."*

The following day, I received the call that would change my life. Metro Lutheran Ministries offered me the position as their Program Coordinator for the Learning to Earn program. I accepted, overwhelmed by the

Chapter Sixteen

grace of God. This wasn't just a job—it was an opportunity to live out my passion and my purpose.

Metro Lutheran Ministries wasn't just an organization; it became a pivotal force in my life. They didn't see my past as a barrier but as a testament to my resilience and strength. Working there opened doors that I never thought possible—doors that only God could unlock. And as I look back on that day, I felt the nudge to turn my car around.I realize that sometimes, all it takes is a moment of obedience to change the course of your entire life.

When I joined Metro Lutheran Ministries, it felt as if I had come full circle. The clients who walked through the doors—those grappling with homelessness, reentry after incarceration, and the turmoil of street life—reminded me of my own journey. I managed each case with a strength-based approach, understanding that true transformation came from recognizing the potential within each person.

Chapter SEVENTEEN

BUILDING P2P MINISTRY: A BEACON OF HOPE

I'll never forget the moment I received that call from the United States Federal Probation Office. It was October 19, 2015. The day was crisp, autumn leaves swirling in the Kansas City breeze, and my heart skipped a beat as I listened to the voice on the other end. They wanted me to share my story at the pretrial orientation program. My story. My journey. It felt like an affirmation, the first real opportunity to take the pain, the struggle, and the redemption I had lived and use it to impact others. This wasn't just a chance—it was a calling.

Standing there in that office in Kansas City, both Kansas and Missouri, felt surreal. The air was thick with the anticipation of those who were about to face the daunting reality of federal incarceration, and I, once in their shoes, was now on the other side, offering something beyond words: hope, understanding, direction. As I

Chapter Seventeen

spoke, my voice steady, I could see the flicker of light in their eyes, a spark that told me they were grasping at the message I was laying down. It wasn't about where they were; it was about where they were going.

As I continued my work with Metro Lutheran Ministry, more doors began to open, like rivers converging into a wider stream. On December 11, 2015, I had another incredible opportunity—this time at University of Missouri Kansas City's (UMKC) law program. The air in the classroom was electric, students perched on the edge of their seats, eager to learn not from books, but from my lived experience. Dr. Rita had given me 75 full minutes, and I used every second of it to dive deep, peeling back the layers of the prison and judicial system, exposing its impact not just on me but on countless families.

I spoke about the humanity often lost in the machinery of justice, the collateral damage no one prepares you for. By the end, the room was silent, not out of disinterest, but because my story had hit them in ways that textbooks never could. They were learning through my scars, my survival.

Then came the unexpected—a phone call from Leavenworth Federal Prison. February 2, 2016, was etched into my mind as another turning point. Walking into the GED program, I wasn't just speaking to men confined by walls but to men standing on the edge of something greater. Warden Maye's feedback after my talk was humbling—he said it was overwhelming, and he meant that in the best possible way. The men resonated with my message: it wasn't about where they were at that moment, but where they were going after the bars opened. My words painted a picture of what could be, and the men latched onto it like a lifeline.

The calls from the United States Probation and Pretrial Services kept coming. They wanted me to speak to those who were about to embark on their federal prison time, to give them a roadmap for navigating the system. I didn't sugarcoat anything—I laid it out as it was. The day-to-day grind, the programs they could engage with, the mental shifts they needed to survive, and, most importantly, how to come out the other side better, not bitter. Even today, they still reach out to me, and each time, it feels like I'm paying forward the grace I was given.

February 18, 2016

Brought me back to USP Leavenworth for their community relations board meeting. The room was filled with decision-makers and leaders, and once again, Warden Maye trusted me to bring a voice of lived experience into the conversation. My incarceration had become a tool for change, not just for myself, but for others who had never walked in those shoes but needed to understand.

Then there was March 15, 2016—Swope Health Services. I walked into the Imani House, an inpatient and outpatient treatment center, and felt an immediate connection with the individuals there. I shared my struggles with drugs and alcohol, and at that time, I could proudly say I had eight years clean and sober. I didn't stand before them as some untouchable success story but as someone who had been in the trenches, who had fought the same demons they were battling. I offered them tools—not just words—but real, practical tools for making it out, for reclaiming their lives once they left

Chapter Seventeen

treatment.

Leavenworth prison called me again, and this time, a chance meeting with a young woman after I spoke sparked something even more profound. She approached me, her eyes wide with recognition. "Are you Stephen Barbee?" she asked. I smiled and nodded. "Yes, I am." She introduced herself as Melissa Bayless, my former unit manager from Pekin, Illinois. The connection was instant, and because of that moment, another opportunity arose. It was as though the universe was aligning, my past meeting my present, opening doors I hadn't even known existed.

These moments, these opportunities, have become threads in a larger tapestry—a tapestry woven from pain, struggle, redemption, and a deep, burning desire to help others see the light beyond their darkest days. Every time I stand before a room full of people, whether at a prison, a probation office, a law class, or a treatment center, I'm reminded that my story isn't just mine. It belongs to all who need to hear it, to those who are still fighting to believe that there's a way forward.

Reflecting on My Journey

Looking back, each opportunity to share my story has been a step further into my purpose. These moments aren't just opportunities for me—they're opportunities for the people I speak to. Whether it's the men in federal prison, future lawyers at UMKC, or individuals in treatment centers, each experience is another chance to speak life into others. I can see the ripple effects, and it humbles me to think that my words, my experiences, and my story could change someone's trajectory.

These are more than just memories—they are milestones of transformation.

Chapter EIGHTEEN

REDEMPTION AND PURPOSE

April 7, 2016

Redemption and purpose will forever be etched in my heart as a day of redemption, restoration, and purpose. As I stood before over 70 Federal Bureau of Prisons staff members at the North Central Regional Office, I couldn't help but marvel at the journey that had brought me to that moment. The same system that once confined me was now offering me a platform to share my story, not as a reminder of my mistakes, but as a testament to God's power to restore and rebuild.

I remember the faces in that room, a mixture of curiosity, skepticism, and interest. These were men and women who had dedicated their lives to law and order, and here I was, once locked up by their colleagues, now standing before them as a guest speaker. There was a

Chapter Eighteen

weight to the moment—a profound sense of irony, but even more so, of grace. God had brought me to this place, to these people, and I knew deep down that my story would matter, that it could spark something.

When Regional Director Sarah Revels handed me a certificate of appreciation, her words stirred something deep within me. "You're an inspiration to my staff," she said, and in that moment, I felt the power of redemption wash over me. Yes, I had made mistakes, served my time, and walked the long road of reentry, but this was living proof that our past doesn't define us. It was a moment to honor the work God had done in me, but more than that, to recognize that my purpose was to give hope to others.

April 26, 2016

I found myself once again stepping into a place of incarceration—this time at USP Leavenworth. Chaplain Hughes had invited me to be part of the Life Connection Program celebration, and I knew that this wasn't just another speaking engagement. It was an opportunity to connect with men who were living the reality I once knew so well.

As I stood before them, I could see the hunger in their eyes—the desire for hope, for freedom, for something greater than the walls around them. I shared my story with them, not just the highs but the lows, the struggles, and the victories that came only by the grace of God. I encouraged them, inspired them, and equipped them with tools to succeed when their time for release came.

Redemption and Purpose

It was these moments—standing in front of prisoners, guards, and staff alike—that continued to shape my calling. My life was now about more than just surviving. It was about thriving in the purpose God had set before me.

January 17, 2017

I began to feel a shift in my spirit. My time at Metro Lutheran Ministries, although filled with growth and service, felt like it was coming to an end. I looked around my office, at the work I had done in the Learning to Earn area, and knew God was calling me to something new. And, as He so often does, God opened the door when Robin from Connections to Success called me.

Her voice on the other end of the phone felt like a divine invitation. "Are you interested in applying for a position with us?" she asked. My heart leapt because this was the kind of work I had been yearning for—work that allowed me to truly live out my calling, to serve people without being held back.

I laughed when she told me what my friend Jeff Lee had said to her. "You can't keep a stallion in a stall," he had told her. Jeff knew me well, knew that I was ready for more. And so, with anticipation, I went in for the interview, though it felt more like a reunion with old friends.

Robin, Katherine, and Brandi were there, and Brandi even remembered hearing me speak years earlier at Leavenworth. That interview was less about questions and answers and more about shared vision, shared hope, and a shared mission. A week later, they offered me the

Chapter Eighteen

position of Community Outreach Manager, and once again, God had opened a door where there had once been a wall.

That role was more than just a title. There was no true job description, so I created one through my actions—reaching out to people at homeless shelters, courts, even bus stops. Wherever there was a need, I was there, connecting people to the resources they needed, giving them a glimpse of the hope and future that was available to them. And as I continued to serve, more opportunities came my way. Speaking engagements at prisons like Ellsworth Correctional Facility in Kansas, Western Missouri Correctional Facility, Crossroads, Western Reception Diagnostic Correctional Center in St. Joseph, and even a return to United States Penitentiary (USP) Springfield Medical Center—all of these were chances to stand before men like me, to tell them that their story didn't have to end in a cell.

I don't take any of these moments lightly. Each one is a divine appointment, a chance to share what God has done in my life, and to remind those who feel forgotten that they are seen, they are valued, and they can rise again. It's not about me. It never has been. It's about the doors God has opened, and the paths He has led me down.

I remember standing at the Fatherhood Conference in Minneapolis, speaking to fathers about the role they play in their children's lives, and then doing the same in Richmond the following year. Each time, I walked away more convinced than ever that God was using me to heal, to inspire, to build bridges where others only saw walls.

Redemption and Purpose

Perhaps one of the most humbling experiences was speaking at the Native American Child Support Conference in San Diego. As I stood before hundreds of Native American leaders and families, I could feel the weight of history, the scars of injustice, and the hope for a better future. It was an honor to share the work of Connections to Success and to speak about how partnerships between courts and social services could transform communities.

All of these opportunities and all of these moments are reminders that God is not done with me. The journey continues, and with every step, I am reminded of His faithfulness, His grace, and His unending love. Every door that opens is a chance to share the story He has written in my life. I give Him all the praise, all the honor, and all the glory, because without Him, none of this would be possible.

July 7, 2014

When I joined Metro Lutheran Ministries, it felt as if I had come full circle. The clients who walked through the doors—those grappling with homelessness, reentry after incarceration, and the turmoil of street life—reminded me of my own journey. I managed each case with a strength-based approach, understanding that true transformation came from recognizing the potential within each person. I wasn't merely connecting them to services; I was seeing them for who they could become, not who they had been. Every meeting with corrections departments or federal prison officials was an opportunity to fight for the forgotten. I made it my mission to provide wrap-around services that would support them in every facet of life—housing, employment, counseling—while reminding them they were more than their past.

Chapter Eighteen

When I became the Community Outreach Manager at Connections to Success in 2017, the puzzle pieces of my life began to form a bigger picture. Speaking at conferences, recruiting volunteers, and building relationships between agencies, I found myself in a position of influence that I could never have imagined. I wasn't just another ex-offender—I was a voice for change, a living testament that redemption was possible. My past no longer felt like a burden but a badge of honor, something I could use to inspire and uplift others.

By the time I stepped into the role of Field Director for Prison Fellowship Ministry in 2021, I knew that my life had been divinely orchestrated for this purpose. I wasn't merely leading programs; I was equipping churches and volunteers to serve the most vulnerable with the same grace that had been extended to me. Every partnership I formed with DOC staff and prison chaplains felt like another step in bridging the gap between a broken system and the people it was meant to rehabilitate. Mobilizing local churches and mentoring volunteers wasn't just work—it was ministry, a chance to demonstrate the love of Christ in a tangible way.

Now, as a court advocate, life coach, and mentor at P2P (Passion to Purpose) Ministry, I walk with others on the same path I once traveled—a path out of darkness. I am no longer the lost man seeking redemption; I am the guide, the mentor, the voice of hope for those who are just beginning their journey. Every day, I establish relationships with court personnel, walk into courtrooms not as a defendant, but as a champion for those seeking a new beginning. I help clients build life plans, connecting them to resources, and showing them that, no matter how far they've fallen, there is always a way back up.

I am more than just a resource specialist. I have become a beacon of hope, walking step by step with people until they are strong enough to walk on their own. The weight I once carried has transformed into purpose, and every life I touch is a testament to the power of grace and the promise of redemption.

Chapter Eighteen

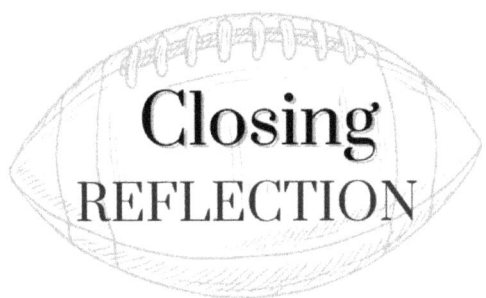

Closing REFLECTION

YOUR PAIN HAS A PULSE LET IT BEAT WITH PURPOSE

You made it.

You've walked with me through the storms, the setbacks, the prison cells—both physical and spiritual. You've seen the pain, the process, and the promise. And now, you stand at the edge of something new not just the last page of this book, but possibly the first page of *your* next chapter.

So let me speak this plainly:
You are more than what happened to you. You are more than your worst day. You are more than your past.

Maybe, like me, you've worn invisible chains for years—chains of addiction, shame, regret, rejection, abandonment, trauma, or the fear of not being enough. Maybe you've been told your story is too messy, too dark, too far gone to matter.

But here's what I've learned:

God does His best work with broken pieces.
Purpose doesn't begin after the pain ends it's *birthed through it.*
Your scars are not signs of defeat they're *evidence that you survived.*

If this book did anything, I hope it gave you permission to be *honest* about your pain and *hopeful* about your future. I hope it cracked open the door for grace to rush in. And I hope it reminded you that your life still matters—*right now*, not just after you "get it all together."

But I also want to challenge you…

Don't let these words sit on the page. Put them into motion. Let your healing turn into helping. Let your pain become a platform. Let your lessons become someone else's lifeline.

Because somebody needs your story.
Somebody is praying for a testimony like yours.
Somebody is silently wondering if they can get through what you just survived.

And you you have the answer.

So don't go back to what broke you. Don't shrink back into silence or settle for surviving. Step boldly into your *assignment*. Not perfection. Not performance. But **purpose** the kind of purpose that's been forged in fire and now shines with hope.

As I close this final page, know that this journey was never just mine it was always meant to awaken yours.

You were born with purpose.
You were wounded for a reason.
You were rescued to reach others.
You are still here because **your assignment is not finished.**

Now go walk it out with courage, with faith, and with the power that comes from knowing:
Your story still matters. And your purpose still lives.

With love, honor, and belief in your journey,
Stephen Barbee

Call or Text:
770-240-0089 Press Extension 1
Web: KLEpub.com
Email Services@klepub.com

It's time to start and finish   YOUR Story!

KLE Publishing specializes in helping people become authors. In as little as 15 to 90 days, we can help you develop your books and e-books and publish to 39,000 outlets! We also offer audiobook services.

Write, Edit, Format, Publish
We can help from
Start to Finish.

Explore and learn more about published authors affiliated with KLE.

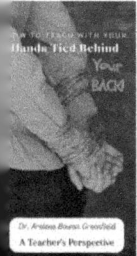

KLEPub.com

www.ingramcontent.com/pod-product-compliance
Lightning Source LLC
Chambersburg PA
CBHW050858240426
43673CB00026B/477/J